Crosscurrents / MODERN CRITIQUES

Harry T. Moore, *General Editor*

STAGES OF THE CLOWN

Perspectives on Modern Fiction From Dostoyevsky to Beckett

Richard Pearce

WITH A PREFACE BY

Harry T. Moore

SOUTHERN ILLINOIS UNIVERSITY PRESS
Carbondale and Edwardsville

FEFFER & SIMONS, INC.
London and Amsterdam

For Jean

Copyright © 1970, by Southern Illinois University Press
All rights reserved
Printed in the United States of America
Designed by Andor Braun
ISBN 0–8093–0449-X
Library of Congress Catalog Card Number 74–86188

Contents

Stages of the Clown: Perspectives on Modern Fiction from Dostoyevsky to Beckett—*the main title, Stages of the Clown, catches one's interest immediately (what could this be?), and the subtitle then gives one the scope of the inquiry, a discussion of imaginative literature going as far back as Fyodor Dostoyevsky (an extremely today-oriented author) and coming up to the chief of our avant-garde, Samuel Beckett. This is a fascinatingly ambitious project, and Richard Pearce has admirably realized its potential.*

Drawing from time to time upon previous commentators, always properly credited, Mr. Pearce essentially goes his own way in this full and rich study of a gallery of modern authors, all of them highly esteemed at this time. I think that Mr. Pearce's insights about them will be widely appreciated.

Look at the twentieth-century authors he draws clown figures from: Saul Bellow, Ralph Ellison, Franz Kafka, Flannery O'Connor, William Faulkner, John Hawkes, Vladimir Nabokov, Günter Grass, and William Burroughs, as well as the previously mentioned Beckett.

In exploring the nineteenth century, Mr. Pearce discusses one other novelist besides Dostoyevsky: Charles Dickens. Dickens too is very much with us today, as we may see from the demonstrations in his favor during the centennial of his birth. Mr. Pearce doesn't choose to deal with all of Dickens' work which might supply us with clowns, but, as in the case of most of these other authors, with one of the books. Surprisingly, this is Great Expectations (which at least stands with Bleak House and The Pickwick Papers at the top of all Dickens' work). Mr. Pearce shows us convincingly how Pip in Great Expectations, like Joseph K. in Kafka's The Trial, represents an alazon, corresponding to the intruder or impostor in Classical literature; what we now often call the alien or outsider. To both Pip and Joseph K., the very landscape is menacing; they are out of harmony with things. In Great Expectations, Mr. Pearce points out, "a multitude of collisions" create the comedy, a comedy which, like that of Faulkner's or Dostoyevsky's or Kafka's, grows out of anxiety.

The Dostoyevsky novel Mr. Pearce selects to talk about is The Idiot. He doesn't see Prince Myshkin as an alazon, but rather as a product of the "fantastic reality" of the Grotesque, another of these Stages of the Clown which this author examines profitably.

By now it must be clear that Mr. Pearce doesn't always pick obviously comic material to discuss: in the case of Faulkner, for example, instead of the Snopes trilogy or something like The Reivers, he takes Light in August, a true tale of horror, but in Mr. Pearce's view an expression of Faulkner's fundamentally comic view of life, which gave him a "form that enabled him to express total irrationality and outrageous violence" as well as "possibilities that were redemptive." Like Kafka's Joseph K., Joe Christmas in Light in August is "a tragic alazon." The book is full of situations that, while not laughable, are ludicrous, and: "The final reference to the circus emphasizes how Faulkner's world makes all human effort ridiculous—and that Byron Bunch, its most attractive and admirable character, will never be more than a buffoon, or fool."

Günter Grass's The Tin Drum makes for easier comic

reference, and the several works of Flannery O'Connor which Mr. Pearce investigates offer us an interesting gallery of Grotesques. Only the other day, in writing the Preface for another new book in this Crosscurrents series—Charles Alva Hoyt's Minor American Novelists—I noticed, in Paul Levine's chapter on Flannery O'Connor, that he mentioned Sherwood Anderson in connection with her use of Grotesques (remember the Prologue to Winesburg, Ohio?), and that he also brought in Saul Bellow, whose Henderson, the Rain King is dealt with in the present volume. And so, as I have said, are works by Samuel Beckett and other present-day authors of importance about whom Mr. Pearce has much to say that is fresh and valid.

So far, this Preface has spoken only about Mr. Pearce's treatment of various authors. Once again, let me say that he has chosen a group of the best possible writers to talk about from the point of view of serious readers today; he doesn't of course include all the fine authors of our time, but his representative list is one no one can complain about, and—once again—his incisive coverage of the work of these writers, relating it to a theme, is most impressive.

I haven't mentioned his historical references, except in using the word he took from Classical literature—alazon. In illustrating the full meaning of that term, Mr. Pearce early in his book provides an interesting summary of Aristophanes' The Clouds. He also tells us about the English Christmas Pantomime of several centuries ago, with its Harlequin and other clowns, and he refers to such famous clowns of history as Grimaldi and the more recent Grock. Groucho Marx and Mack Sennett are also mentioned, as well as Federico Fellini.

Of course the mingling of the comic and the tragic is no new thing. True, French audiences of Racine's time didn't want clowns in their tragic plays, but the hearty audiences at Shakespeare's Bankside did: even Hamlet, for all his tragic side (and he knew what tragedy was, as his speech to Horatio about "the stamp of one defect" indicates), was highly comic, also, and knew it—as Jules Laforgue did, too.

Mr. Pearce is above mentioning such examples of brummagem as I Pagliacci, but that gaudy verismo opera has long provided one of the great popular examples of the sobbing clown. A current German novelist of far higher stature as an artist than Leoncavallo—Heinrich Böll—has given us a better version of the situation with his recent novel, The Clown. And there are other examples: not many years ago, Leonid Andreyev's He Who Gets Slapped had its successes on stage and screen.

Mr. Pearce generally takes older examples, such as the poem from the medieval Carmina Burana, cited in European Literature and the Latin Middle Ages, by Ernst Robert Curtius (1948). This poem, partly quoted in Curtius' book (Mr. Pearce's treatment of the verses appears in the present volume on p. 84), shows what Curtius called "The world upsidedown," a phrase which Mr. Pearce adapts for two chapters of his book. Curtius, in his full study of a definite period, of course traces this upsidedownness thoroughly, showing that although the poem in question is essentially medieval, its origins may be found as far back as what the Greeks called adynata, the juxtaposition of "impossibilities," perhaps first used by Archilochus in 648 B.C. The method continued to be used: "The Virginial adynata were known in the Middle Ages," Curtius tells us.

Another of the many authors Mr. Pearce has usefully consulted for his historical background is J. Huizinga, late Rector of the University of Leiden, and author of one of the finest books on late-medieval France and the Netherlands, The Waning of the Middle Ages (1924). Mr. Pearce doesn't cite this volume, which deals with the grimness of life in that period, particularly as represented by the Totentanz in theatrical performances, poems, and woodcuts; but Mr. Pearce does refer to Huizinga's other remarkable book, Homo Ludens: A Study of the Play Element in Culture (1938), which has many valuable contributions to make to the subject we are just now interested in, particularly in the chapter, "Play-Forms in Art." Huizinga throughout his book refers to Plato, and closes his chapter on "The Elements of Myth-opoesis" with a reference to the Symposium.

The reader will remember the situation at the end of that Dialogue. Almost everyone had gone to sleep after drinking too much liquor, but at dawn Aristodemus woke up to find Socrates talking to two friends: "Aristodemus [in the Jowett translation] was only half awake, and he did not hear the beginning of the discourse; the chief thing which he remembered was Socrates compelling the other two to acknowledge that the genius of comedy was the same as that with tragedy, and that the true artist in comedy was an artist in tragedy also. To this they were constrained to consent, being drowsy, and not quite following the argument." Interestingly, Huizinga didn't quite follow it either, for in Homo Ludens he stated, "The true poet, says Socrates in Plato's Symposium, must be tragic and comic at once, and the whole of human life must be felt as a blend of tragedy and comedy." That last clause doesn't belong to Socrates' discourse. Nevertheless, we can accept it as an implication.

We have been for a while in the historical past; but that is a tribute to Richard Pearce's fine book, which invokes it. He shows us at once how traditional so many of our fine recent and contemporary writers are, and at the same time he reveals to us how fresh and exciting their work really is.

HARRY T. MOORE

Southern Illinois University
May 1, 1970

Acknowledgments

In pursuing this study over the past five years I have been indebted to the Alfred University Research Foundation and the American Council of Learned Societies for financial support during the summers of 1963 and 1967, and to the Administration, English Department colleagues, and students of Wheaton College for their valuable encouragement and criticism. I am also indebted to a number of people whom I have never met, but whose books or lectures have opened my mind to new ways of experiencing modern literature: Wolfgang Kayser in *The Grotesque in Art and Literature*; Enid Welsford in *The Fool: His Social and Literary History*; Jan Kott in *Shakespeare Our Contemporary*; Frederick Hoffman in *The Mortal No: Death and the Modern Imagination*; Michel Foucault in *Madness and Civilization: A History of Insanity in the Age of Reason*; Johan Huizinga in *Homo Ludens: A Study of the Play Element in Culture*; Victor Ehrlich in his lecture at Brown University on "Gogol and the Grotesque Imagination"; Ihab Hassan in his writing and lectures that took final form in *The Literature of Silence: Henry Miller and Samuel Beckett*. The most profound influence on my thinking came indirectly from Mark Epstein, under whose sensitive and patient tutelage I studied mime in 1966; he taught me to understand—and to feel—the kind of dramatic activity that has led to my final conclusions about the function and the value of the clown.

xiv   Acknowledgments

A condensed version of "Which Way Is Up?" was read
to the Modern Language Association in 1966, and parts
of the chapter on Flannery O'Connor to the New England College English Association in 1967. I would like to
thank the following publications for allowing me to re-
publish, in revised form, other sections of this book:
The Massachusetts Review for "The Walker: Modern
American Hero" (Summer 1964); *Wisconsin Studies in
Contemporary Literature* for "Faulkner's One Ring
Circus" (Autumn 1966); and *Masterplots* for essay-
reviews of Ralph Ellison's *Invisible Man* and Flannery
O'Connor's *Everything That Rises Must Converge*.

I would especially like to thank Curtis Dahl, Jane
Lewin, Stephen Lottridge, Barry Knower, Edwin Briggs,
and Earl Rovit for their criticism of my manuscript.
Finally, I would like to thank my wife, Jean, for the
reading and rereading, the criticizing and arguing, the
generosity, and the inspiration for carrying through this
clownish enterprise.

RICHARD PEARCE

Wheaton College
Norton, Massachusetts
1968

Stages of the Clown

1

Stages of the Clown

Stages of the Clown has three major bases: first, that in
the line of fiction running from Dostoyevsky through
Beckett the most terrifying and exhilarating experiences
are based—in form and meaning—on comic structures;
second, that these experiences are evoked by means that
are principally visual and dramatic; and third, that important words like "absurd," "grotesque," and "clown,"
now unfortunately glib and trite, refer to experiences,
forms, and characters of great variety. It is the purpose of
this book to explore what we have come to accept as a
compelling and relevant modern trend from the various
perspectives of the ancient clown tradition. The book is
designed to reach out rather than to encompass, to pro-
voke discussion rather than to complete it. The "stages"
of the title refer to the different levels of the clown's
development, although I do not wish to imply any sense
of progress, and also to the different worlds he inhabits;
for we should remember that the clown is a native of the
stage, not the book.

Let me emphasize that although this book is histori-
cally oriented it is not historical, although it is wide-rang-
ing it is not comprehensive. At the center of my study is
an archetypal world that is at once fearfully demonic and
abundantly potent. Such a world is not amenable to
scrutiny through the well-polished lenses of rationalistic
scholarship, but it may be refracted, and in this way
known, through the proper prism. The unifying principle of this book, then, is that of a multifaceted prism.

The critical method is one of radical perspectives. In each chapter I explore a very small group of modern works, even a single work, from a different facet of the same prism; that is from one radical perspective, or stage, of the clown's world. In each chapter I also explore a stage of the clown's world or the clown himself on one of these stages, and the modern works have been chosen with this end in view. With the exception of Flannery O'Connor, whose works have a unique integrity, I have limited myself to one or two works of an author, for references or allusions to other works in their canons would require blurring qualifications. For the same reason I have subordinated or eschewed chronology, cultural and literary influences, and cross-references to analogous works. There is no question that there are important books in the modern tradition that I have not found a way to explore, just as there are stages of the clown's world that I have not discovered. My study will succeed in one respect if it stimulates the reader to examine other works from other facets of the same prism.

The grotesque stage, the world of the clown, and the means used to evoke this world are the main, although not exclusive, subjects of the first three chapters. In *The Idiot* and "The Metamorphosis" Dostoyevsky and Kafka create worlds where men are gratuitously transformed into clownish puppets. The techniques used to create these worlds and the meaning of each literary experience can be better understood if we relate them to the techniques and experiences of the silent film, the vaudeville stage, and, one important origin for them both, the Transformation Scene of the English Christmas Pantomime. In *Great Expectations* and *The Trial* Dickens and Kafka show us man as an intruder in the very world in which he is compelled to live; the theme of intrusion is dramatized in startling ways that can be explored by recalling the archetypal intruder, the *alazon* of classical comedy. *The Idiot* and "The Metamorphosis" picture man defeated or made irrelevant by transcendent powers; *Great Expectations* and *The Trial* show man comically but tragically expelled by immanent forces. *Light in August* shows man at the ridiculous mercy of forces that are at once transcendent and immanent. Faulkner creates his stage as a chessboard, where the pattern is simultaneously deterministic and absurdly comic, where Joe Christmas is drawn into and excluded from society, where he is forced to choose an identity and denied the opportunity, where heroic action is inevitably clownish. Faulkner's view of life and art is fundamentally more comic than that of Dostoyevsky or Kafka, and he ends his novel with a realization of the values of comedy and clownishness: Byron Bunch in the tradition of the buffoon innocently affirms all the values abrogated in the major part of the novel.

The second part of this study focuses more on the clown than on his world. In using the term "clown" I am following Enid Welsford in her sensitive and comprehensive study of *The Fool: His Social and Literary History*. Miss Welsford uses the terms clown and fool interchangeably. She states that "the Fool or Clown is the Comic Man, but he is not necessarily the hero of comedy, the central figure about whom the story is told, nor is he a mere creature of the poetic imagination whom the final drop-curtain consigns to oblivion. . . . As a dramatic character he usually stands apart from the main action of the play, having a tendency not to focus but to dissolve events, and also to act as an intermediary between the stage and the audience. As an historical figure he does not confine his activities to the theater but makes everyday life comic on the spot. The Fool, in fact, is an amphibian, equally at home in the world of reality and the world of the imagination. . . . The serious hero focuses events, forces issues, and causes catastrophes; but the Fool by his mere presence dissolves events, evades issues, throws doubt on the finality of fact." I prefer to use "clown" as the generic term which includes varieties of fools, buffoons, tricky devils, and Harlequin figures, because it throws more emphasis on the grotesque world he inhabits. And in pursuing his development into modern literature, I shall try to show what happens when he becomes central to the action and still retains the ability to "dissolve events" and "throw doubt on the finality of fact." Flannery O'Connor uses the clown to turn the world upside down. Through one inversion she startles us into fresh views of contemporary reality; through a second inversion she rediscovers essential truths, transvalues values, and affirms a primal order. She follows in the tradition of Plato and Erasmus, who used their clowns, Socrates and Folly, to play the same kind of game. But turning the world upside down can be played toward still another end, as it was by the clownish demons of the medieval miracle plays and the fools of the *sottie* drama—an apocalyptic but vital destruction. William Burroughs tries to achieve this kind of destruction. And Nabokov, in *Lolita*, succeeds in shattering the world as we know it, leaving us profoundly disturbed and at the same time exhilarated by the joy of his destructiveness.

Like the medieval demons and fools, Harlequin thrives in chaos but is not finally a destroyer. He is as affirmative as Socrates and Folly, but he lacks their faith in a primal order. He is as innocent as the buffoon, but he is sharply aware of himself and his absurd and menacing situation. Saul Bellow's *Henderson the Rain King* and John Hawkes's *Second Skin* with their complementary bases in social and psychological reality are well suited to explore the personality of the clown who accepts his role in an absurd world. The clown who not only accepts but actively chooses his role is traced to what appears to be the very limit in Ralph Ellison's *Invisible Man,* Günter Grass's *Tin Drum,* and Samuel Beckett's trilogy.

The conclusion is an attempt to draw out some of the meanings of the Grotesque experience and some of the values of the clown tradition. The final exploration leads back to the origins of Greek comedy, and into the basic principles of improvisation. It relates Beckett's prose style to the epitome of improvisation, that of the mime, who carves meanings out of pure silence and pure space. Finally, the conclusion is an attempt to connect the clown tradition as it has developed in modern literature to an important strand of humanism which shows man, confronted with the stark menace and the great potential of absolute freedom, stringing together impossibilities, creating and destroying and creating to no end other than his own joy, with full awareness of his own precarious situation and of the evanescent but nonetheless affirmative values of his clownish creations.

2

Transformation
Dostoyevsky's *Idiot* and Kafka's "Metamorphosis"

The English Christmas Pantomime of the eighteenth century began with a fairy tale, in dialogue, song, and dance; at the climax of the fairy tale the Queen would transform all the characters into the people of the Harlequinade—Harlequin, Clown, Pantaloon, Columbine, and others. The Transformation Scene, a Cecil B. De Mille extravaganza of its day, would destroy the reality of the fairy-tale world, which was already a world of the imagination. The Harlequinade was totally irrelevant to the fairy tale and was played in an entirely different key; it consisted of fifteen to twenty unrelated scenes that changed in rapid-fire succession. In a single play Harlequin would flit in and out of them with his magic sword, causing characters to fly out of their seats and birds to fly out of pies, changing people into clocks, sideboards into beehives, benches into traps, creating gold for the poor, making tables ascend and multiply and be filled with delicacies. In the early nineteenth century, when Grimaldi put on the greasepaint and costume of Clown, Harlequin moved out of stage center. But Clown's success was due to a revitalization of Harlequin's tricks. The act with which Clown enchanted all of London has been called a "construction." He would transform the pots and barrels of an alehouse into soldiers, and review them in a saucepan and a dish cover. He would dress a corpse in a bear's skin, swan's feathers, and an ass's head, and then bring the new-formed beast to life. He would turn Pantaloon into a wheelbarrow by handing him a mop stick thrust through a cheese and lifting him by the heels.

The key to the Christmas Pantomime, then, was its power of transformation. The splendor of the fairy tale, the mechanics of the Transformation Scene, the rapid chaotic pace of the Harlequinade, the tricks of Harlequin, the constructions of Clown—all made the real world more and more remote to an audience that was already enjoying a holiday. But more, starting with the Transformation Scene, it gave the spectators a heightened awareness of the relation between man and the objects of his world.

Grimaldi succeeded by endowing objects with a peculiar vitality. And a hundred years later the famous Swiss clown, Grock, recalled in his memoirs how "all kinds of inanimate objects have had a way of looking at me reproachfully and whispering to me in unguarded moments: 'We've been waiting for you . . . take us now, and turn us into something different.' " While the clown was revealing a gay vitality in the mechanical world, he was approaching the border of terror, for in just one more step he could disclose what Friedrich Vischer called "the malice of the inanimate object." When the inanimate object is endowed with a malicious power, it appears to usurp the vitality of the human character, in fact to transform the human character into a mechanical puppet. It is just this transformation that Henri Bergson, in his essay on "Laughter," claims is the source of comedy—we laugh when we see *something mechanical encrusted on the living,*" when a human being, normally distinguished by his resiliency and adaptability, suddenly appears to be rigid or to act out of sheer momentum. Even when this transformation is effected by a malicious power it has a strong comic potency. In such a transformation, however, the comedy shocks us into experiencing the menace of the absurd.

Comedy, then, has the power of destroying our everyday world with opposite results. Wolfgang Kayser in a definitive study, *The Grotesque in Art and Literature*, shows how the Grotesque, which took its name from the fanciful and bizarre style of paintings discovered in Italian grottoes in the fifteenth century, developed along two paths—one through the playful, gay, and fantastic world of the *commedia dell'arte*; and the other through the underground and sinister world of dreams. But the two paths were always connected. Depending on an essentially comic destruction of the everyday world, they were two different manifestations of the same absurd experience.

In the early movies comedy and terror were blended through cinematic techniques for bringing objects to life and turning people into things; further, the sped-up and silent action contributed to the mechanical transformation. Charlie Chaplin trying to balance a shack that had slipped to the edge of a cliff, Buster Keaton fighting with a deck chair and matching wits with a railroad engine, the voiceless Harpo Marx producing giant scissors and a klaxon horn from bottomless pockets, recall the theatrics of Grock and Grimaldi. But the film's realism added a new dimension. Sitting in the dark the spectator becomes totally absorbed in the movie, and is unaware of the camera tricks and film editing; thus the transformation is believable. We respond with laughter when the transformation breaks the realistic mood enough to effect detachment. If we remain absorbed, however, we react with terror to the destruction of a realistic world into which we have been drawn. It is on just this point that Kayser made a distinction between Comedy and the Grotesque: in Comedy we are detached from the world that is being destroyed; in the Grotesque we are drawn into it, and all bases for stability and security are annihilated. We might modify Kayser's point, however, for in some of the most exhilarating esthetic experiences, especially those of the early films, we are simultaneously detached and involved; and our response is a mixture, in sometimes disturbing proportions, of joy and terror.

After the film, prose fiction is the most effective medium for evoking a realistic experience, and the writer can employ variations of cinematic techniques. Robbe-Grillet, consciously influenced by the film, would have the modern novelist view objects not as props for human characters but as things in themselves. Dostoyevsky and Kafka, although they did not consciously utilize techniques of the cinema or the pantomime stage, were both drawn to Dickens, a master of comic techniques and the biographer of Grimaldi. The fictional worlds of Dostoyevsky and Kafka acquire their special qualities largely from the surprising ways these authors revived the tradition that went back to the Transformation Scene in the English Christmas Pantomime.

From the perspective of the Transformation Scene let us explore Dostoyevsky's *Idiot* and Kafka's "Metamorphosis." The noble and Christ-like Myshkin is turned into a hopeless idiot, the sensitive Gregor into a horrible insect. We respond to *The Idiot* and "The Metamorphosis" with a despair that derives from seeing human beings denied their humanity, and, more strikingly, with an outrage that results from witnessing in startling detail a gratuitous transformation of the human into the sub-human, and ultimately into the nonhuman. Each transformation is indeed tragic, but it is achieved by the very same kind of low-comic devices that I have been discussing. It is the comic surprise that annihilates the distinction between the human and nonhuman worlds. And it is the device of the low-comic stage or screen that evokes the gratuitous transformation.

Dostoyevsky and Kafka effect the transformation by

techniques that are essentially visual and dramatic. The transformation scene itself becomes what in the classical dramatic plot is the reversal or peripety. In *The Idiot* the peripety occurs near the end of the novel at the climactic party which Mme Epanchin gives to celebrate the engagement of her daughter Aglaia to Prince Myshkin. She has invited the best society, to whom Myshkin has not yet been introduced; and Aglaia with a mixture of sympathetic forethought and mischievous anticipation, has warned the Prince to avoid animated argument and wild gesticulation—and, most importantly, to watch out for the precious vase. But, enchanted by the company and absorbed in the discussion, Myshkin forgets himself and moves to the armchair right next to the great piece of china:

At his last words he suddenly rose from his seat, and incautiously waved his arm, somehow twitching his shoulder and . . . there was a general scream of horror! The vase tottered at first, as though hesitating whether to fall upon the head of some old gentleman, but suddenly inclining in the opposite direction, towards the German poet, who skipped aside in alarm, it crashed to the ground. A crash, a scream, and the priceless fragments were scattered about the carpet, dismay and astonishment—what was Myshkin's condition would be hard, and is perhaps unnecessary, to describe! But we must not omit to mention one odd sensation, which struck him at that very minute, and stood out clearly above the mass of other confused and strange sensations. It was not the shame, not the scandal, not the fright, nor the suddenness of it that impressed him most, but his foreknowledge of it! He could not explain what was so arresting about that thought, he only felt that it had gripped him to the heart, and he stood still in a terror that was almost superstitious! Another instant and everything seemed opening out before him; instead of horror there was light, joy, and ecstasy; his breath began to fail him, and . . . but the moment had passed. Thank God, it was not that! He drew a breath and looked about him.

Myshkin is so engrossed in his argument that he forgets Aglaia's admonition and ignores the nearby vase. Gesticulating like an automaton, he falls into the class of comic characters described by Bergson who act out of inertia, and who create the sudden and ludicrous impression of something mechanical encrusted on the living. Myshkin's humanity has been established in innumerable scenes illustrating his sensibility and compassion. Further, his argument has been about the Russian urge for extremes, which, like Underground Man's response to being considered a piano key, is a gesture of revolt and freedom, the ultimate human affirmation against the mechanical. But Myshkin's humanity is abrogated by an unexpected mechanization of the scene. This is accomplished through a shift from intellectual discourse to physical description, from sound to sight. It is like a cinematic device where the sounds of human voices are suddenly erased, leaving only what appears to be irrelevant physical action and the noise of objects. Hence the gratuitous and farcical effect of something mechanical encrusted on the living.

Does the comic device ridicule Myshkin and his ideas? I think not, for the scene finally shows Myshkin to be more valuable and fragile than the vase he smashes. Such a sympathetic view of Myshkin may be due to still another shift, this time in perspective. In traditional comedy we are not permitted to identify with the person being ridiculed; we view the scene from a world that the comic butt has at least temporarily abandoned. However, in the middle of Dostoyevsky's description, the perspective is shifted from without to within the protagonist. "A crash, a scream, and the priceless fragments were scattered about the carpet, dismay and astonishment—what was Myshkin's condition . . ." and what follows is a complex record of Myshkin's psychological response. The sudden mechanization of the scene connects Myshkin's radical alienation and ridiculous fate with an arbitrary mechanical force. When we are drawn into Myshkin's mind we feel his alienation; the mechanical force becomes a threat to our own mental and emotional security.

As Myshkin recovers, he seems "for a long time unable to understand the fuss that was going on around him, or rather, he understood it perfectly and saw everything, but stood, as it were apart, as though he had no share in it, and, like someone invisible in a fairy tale, had crept into the room and was watching people, with whom he had no concern though they interested him." He sees people picking up pieces of the vase, hears rapid conversation, watches Aglaia's strange expression, and finally is startled to discover that everyone has sat down and is laughing as if nothing had happened. Again Dostoyevsky is creating an effect by means of a device that we can now explain by reference to stage and film techniques. In the final scene of Ionesco's *Bald Soprano*, the characters turn pieces of nonsensical syntax into bludgeons. In all of Harold Pinter's plays the characters turn clichés into instruments of torture. Both playwrights create an atmosphere of menace by disengaging conventional meanings from the auditory and visual experience. In Fellini's movie 8½ a man is caught in a traffic jam behind the electrically closed windows of his automobile. During his futile struggle to escape, the camera turns to the various characters in the other cars; they are all unaware of the victim's plight, and the sequence is absolutely silent. The noise of the man pounding within the car, interrupted by the silence without, evokes an extraordinary sense of menace, which is very much like Ionesco's and Pinter's. But Fellini has gone a step beyond the playwrights—he has disengaged sound from sight. And this is just what Dostoyevsky accomplishes within the far greater limits of his prose medium. By creating a continuity of the visual accompanied by the discontinuity of the auditory, he makes the medium itself assume the role of Fate, capriciously transforming the protagonist into a ridiculous victim.

With Aglaia's warning, the day before the party, the vase became endowed with value and power, and Myshkin sensed that he would be responsible for its destruction. Throughout the novel all values and ideas are reversed, despite Dostoyevsky's initial intention; it becomes more and more difficult to tell good from evil, sanity from madness. In the climactic scene the object and the human change places. The awful and pathetic comedy of this exchange is realized when we view Myshkin's epileptic seizure and see him as a helpless puppet. But this is not the end for Myshkin, for he is not only transformed by the arbitrary mechanical power, he is made to join forces with it. In the scenes that follow, which become more and more formally comic, we see Myshkin as more and more destructive.

If the Epanchin party contains the climax and the peripety, the falling action begins in the next chapter, where Myshkin is forced to decide between Aglaia and Nastasya. Here inevitability and absurdity are heightened by a form which begins as melodrama and ends as farce. The scene is set in the house where Nastasya and Rogozhin have been staying. Aglaia enters escorted by Myshkin. As the two men fade into the background, the two women, who meet for the first time and draw together two important themes, confront each other with confessions and accusations. They become hysterical, and finally, ignoring the handsome and heroic Rogozhin, fight for exclusive possession of the passive, unattractive Myshkin. Aglaia, affronted by Myshkin's momentary hesitation, stalks off. Myshkin, in the fashion of a courtier, begins to follow. But he is stopped at the door as Nastasya falls senselessly into his arms, and the chapter ends with Myshkin "soothing and comforting her like a child."

The argument between Aglaia and Nastasya is psychologically revealing; Dostoyevsky handles the melodramatic situation so as to maximize the emotional potentialities and develops the two women as fully human characters. But he also transforms the melodrama into a farce, with a geometrical balancing of male and female counterparts, a desperate argument over the most unlikely prize, mistaken intentions, and switching of partners. As the two women contest Myshkin like Solomon's plaintiff harlots, they turn him from a melodramatic hero into a slapstick puppet. They also force upon him an absurd choice—since he must choose one of them, he must humiliate the other; and since he is a puppet, he can satisfy neither. The grotesque joke of the farce is that Myshkin is denied the opportunity to choose.

The turning of melodrama into farce first focuses our attention on action, then underscores the inevitability of action, and finally makes a mockery of action altogether. Ironically, this scene is of utmost importance in the plot line. And this is emphasized by the radical shift in the narrator's stance in the beginning of the next chapter, a singular tactic for Dostoyevsky, even considering the problems of serialization. For more than five hundred pages the narrator has been omniscient, free to move in and out of the minds of all the characters, in full possession of all the facts. Now he begins: "A fortnight had passed since the events narrated in the last chapter, and the positions of the persons concerned were so completely changed that it is extremely difficult for us to continue our story without certain explanations. And yet we must, as far as possible, confine ourselves to the bare statement of facts and for a very simple reason: because we find it difficult in many instances to explain what occurred." The scene that was so vividly described in the previous chapter has suddenly become remote. It is as if the narrator and reader have not been witnesses but must depend upon the conflicting speculations of the townspeople, which involve politics, religion, and the enigma of who was the "lost woman" and who seduced whom. The narrator confesses that he can give no explanation of motives or meanings, and insists that we be satisfied by the simple facts: a marriage has been arranged between Myshkin and Nastasya, and it will be entirely in the hands of the buffoons who began by exploiting Myshkin and have ended by being his only friends. In his notebooks for *The Idiot*, Dostoyevsky states, "We admit that we are about to describe strange happenings—Since it is difficult to explain them, let us confine ourselves to facts." But why this sudden shift in artistic strategy, and why here? He tries to articulate his reasons, "We recognize that nothing different could have happened to the Idiot"; and then further on: "Reality above everything. It is true perhaps that we have a different conception of reality, a thousand thoughts, prophecy—a fantastic reality. It may be that in the Idiot man is visible in a truer light." The radical shift does contribute to this "fantastic reality," and does make man visible in a new light. The narrator's unexpected change in perspective and tone contributes to the suspense, allowing him to add more incidents than the novel would otherwise bear; more importantly, it heightens the comic confusion, and removes the reader from the situation in which he had been caught up by the early melodrama. But we are still carried along by the inertia of our previous involvement in the story, and we therefore continue to follow the action with a double point of view. In the end, Dostoyevsky's melodrama with its undercurrent of genuine tragedy and farce is held in a suspension, as it were, of the Grotesque. This is the fantastic reality.

The two major scenes in the two concluding chapters are as funny as anything conceived by Mack Sennett or Groucho Marx, and unless we recognize the slapstick and laugh at it, we are denied their full and unsettling experience. The ex-prizefighter, Keller, upon hearing that he will be Myshkin's best man, "raised his right hand, with the forefinger apart from the rest, and cried, as though taking a vow: 'I won't drink.'" Then, "in anticipation of a great rush of thirsty souls on coming out of the church," he advises Myshkin "to have the fire-hose ready in the courtyard." The sycophant, Lebedyev, is opposed, for he envisions the crowd tearing the house to pieces; and an argument ensues in which Keller accuses Lebedyev of intriguing against Myshkin. The roughhouse, confusion, comic intrigue, all foreshadow the wedding scene itself; and the narrator, having lapsed back into omniscience for several pages, once again becomes scrupulous about his evidence: "The account of what followed at the wedding was given me by people who saw it all, and I think it is correct."

Lebedyev has invited a doctor because of the "order on his breast." Keller, with an "undisguised inclination for combat . . . cast very hostile looks at the sightseers." The crowd boos and cheers—and then stands petrified as Rogozhin appears from nowhere, and, responding to Nastasya's passionate request, sweeps her into his arms, his carriage, and a departing train. The brief melodrama evokes a sense of unexpected and unnecessary violence. But suddenly, as in the previous chapter, the melodrama is turned into farce: the pugnacious Keller pleads that he was taken by surprise, the faithful Burdovsky rationalizes that the Prince would not wish them to fly in pursuit, and Myshkin invites the jeering crowd to a party.

I have emphasized the slapstick dimension of this chapter, first as a corrective to the more common readings that are limited to tragedy, melodrama, and pathos, but also to show that the scene is structurally and essentially farcical. There is no doubt that Myshkin emerges as helpless and isolated, that a beautiful ideal is being mocked and destroyed, that our final response is one of sadness and not joy. But Myshkin's fragility and isolation are evoked by action that is incongruously slapstick. The other characters, who have been portrayed throughout the novel as very much alive, are turned into stereotypes and caricatures, mechanical puppets. Again, it is as if the medium itself has assumed the role of Fate, or at least obscured the true nature of Fate, and we sense that Myshkin is being defeated by a power that is capricious, irrelevant, and nonhuman. Further, this power has turned Myshkin into a puppet who is not only ridiculous in his incongruous action but an agent of destruction. When Myshkin is senselessly forced to choose Nastasya over Aglaia, he drives Aglaia, as Murray Krieger points out, into the arms of a phony Polish nobleman and into the embrace of the Catholic Church—on both counts, for Dostoyevsky, a mark of damnation. When Myshkin is forced into a wedding with Nastasya, he drives her into the arms of a lover who can only be her murderer.

The final scene also begins as melodrama and ends as farce. After a long and suspenseful search Myshkin feels someone in the crowd touch his elbow and whisper his name, "Follow me, brother, I want you." The important theme of "the double," which has been studied for its psychological revelations, is also a variation of traditional comedy's mirroring of characters. The good man and the bad man, the man of love and the man of passion, who met by accident in the opening pages, and who as their paths crossed and recrossed became more of a threat to each other, are finally united. And how? In a scene so ridiculous as to be impossible in the hands of anyone but Dostoyevsky. Rogozhin leads Myshkin through his dark house to the curtained bed and shows him the murdered Nastasya. There is nothing to do now but wait: "We'll stay the night here together," says Rogozhin, sealing the bond of their brotherhood and complicity. "There is no bed but that one, and I thought we might take the pillows off the two sofas and make up a bed here for you and me beside the curtain." So in this large house with all the sofas and chairs, the two men spend the night together alongside the murdered woman. After agreeing "not to give her up on any account to any one," Rogozhin reveals his plan to disguise the smell of death with American leather, Zhdanov's disinfectant, and his mother's flowers; Myshkin responds with queries about a knife and a deck of cards. And when the authorities arrive they witness a parody of the scene concluding Nastasya's victory over Aglaia: they find Myshkin caressing the raving Rogozhin. Now Myshkin has reverted permanently to a state of idiocy.

In this chapter we begin by feeling suspense and terror, and end by feeling pity, emptiness, despair. The concluding emotions result from Dostoyevsky's subversion of comedy. Out of context the bed scene might remind us of A Night at the Opera, but it also might recall the heath scene in King Lear. Shakespeare too was audacious in his use of comedy, and while Jan Kott may obscure important dimensions, his major points about the kind of comedy in King Lear and the kind of universe Lear inhabits are germane. In both The Idiot and King Lear the line between sanity and madness is blurred; in both works we watch the protagonist act contrary to normal expectations (hence the parody and farce) because the workings of the normal world have become senseless and intolerable. Both Dostoyevsky and Shakespeare evoke the full terror of their worlds with comic devices: the mirroring of characters and plots, exaggerated situations, incongruous action—and finally, in Dostoyevsky's bed scene and Shakespeare's scene with the dead Cordelia, a travesty on the marriage ritual that ends traditional comedy. The travesty is the ultimate subversion, for it turns comedy against itself. We comprehend that reconciliation is impossible, that harmony is a nostalgic dream, that we have been seeing life not as a temporary aberration, but as it is.

Lest we carry the comparison too far, we should remember that Shakespeare begins and ends his play with a king, dignified and respected, while Dostoyevsky begins his novel with a fool and ends it with an idiot, pathetic and nearly anonymous. The important difference is that Lear becomes a fool to triumph over a world that is mad and mechanistic; he becomes a better and greater man in the struggle, and his greatness is recognized. But Myshkin is turned from a fool to a puppet; he is good from the very beginning, but his goodness leads to the destruction of Aglaia, Nastasya, and Rogozhin. And while Mme Epanchin sounds a note of sympathy and respect from early in the novel to its very conclusion, it is important to remember that it is only a minor note in the final discord, that what is finally recognized is Myshkin's impotence.

When we turn to Kafka's "Metamorphosis" we enter a world where, in contrast to Shakespeare's and Dostoyevsky's, there is no contest between the protagonist and the mad mechanizing forces; the protagonist is not defeated but made irrelevant.

We may read "The Metamorphosis" as a *psychomachia*, an objectification of a battle within the complex mind of a modern man. Or we may read it as a picture of life shaped by the complex consciousness of a modern man. And inevitably we move our critical focus back and forth between the mind of the character and the mind of the creator. Hence one critic will see Gregor Samsa's transformation as a mark of his living death, and another will see it as a fantasy of the repressed and father-dominated Kafka. But there is a totally different way of reading Kafka. We can view his remarkable fantasies as dramatic objectifications of the world *without* and not the world *within*. We can see the protagonist not as a victim of his own guilt or of his creator's Oedipus complex, but of an absurd and terrifying universe. With Kafka's third person narrator we have no way of telling whether we are focusing on the mind of the protagonist, which distorts objective action, or the objective action itself, which includes the responses of the protagonist. Dorrit Cohn, in her sensitive and closely argued study of "Narrated Monologue: Definition of a Fictional Style," shows how "the temporal and spatial indicators of direct discourse" in Kafka's *erlebte Rede,* or "narrated monologue," locate the point of view within Gregor Samsa's psyche. But when she compares Kafka's technique to that of Henry James, she forgets that James clearly distinguishes the narrator's voice from the voice of his protagonist through a sophisticated irony, and that he distinguishes the subjective from the objective by a controlled use of the dramatic scene. In Kafka the viewpoint is very much limited to the mind of Gregor, but neither the narrator's tone nor the shift from narration to dramatic scene reveals additional information or judgment. The nature of Kafka's work demands that our focus be directed on either the mind of the protagonist or on his world. There is nothing in the story that tells of the relation between the two.

Extending the thesis of Wylie Sypher's *Loss of the Self in Modern Literature and Art,* we could say that the first kind of reading, which sees the work as a projection or product of Gregor's mind, is based on a Romantic assertion of the ego; while the second kind of reading, which views the work as a representation of Gregor's world, is consonant with what Sypher calls the modern humanism, where the ego is displaced, and the scientist and artist no longer view the self as the center of the universe. If the second view of Kafka is due to a recent shift in orientation, we should remember that Kafka himself was largely responsible for this shift, especially in his story of Gregor Samsa's transformation.

We must begin with the fact that we never see Gregor in human form. We have no basis for measuring or judging the change; we have no way of knowing whether the story is dream or reality. After Gregor awakens he examines his situation: he is aware of his transformation and troubled by it, but his immediate concern is for his job and his family. The incongruity is another reversal of Bergson's formula for comedy, since Gregor is an insect but behaves like a man. Nevertheless the result is equally ludicrous. Although critics agree that there are elements of black humor in Kafka, comic readings are rare because of the traditionally subjective orientation or because Kafka's skillful realism causes the reader to identify with the protagonist. But in reading Kafka, and Dostoyevsky, the subordination of the comic is an evasion of the full terror. The classical canon of decorum establishes a measure of security; in a simple world one can fear what is threatening and laugh at what makes one feel happy or superior. The writers we are discussing deny us this simplicity.

With a locked door between them, the chief clerk reprimands Gregor, "You seem bent on making a disgraceful exhibition of yourself." Gregor replies with assurance, "I'm just going to open the door this very minute." The chief clerk cannot understand Gregor, and, more importantly, he cannot see Gregor, who, although not bent on it, is a more disgraceful exhibition than the chief clerk could ever imagine. And Gregor is ridiculously blind to himself when he speaks as if he were not a huge insect and could just open the door and go out as a salesman. The comedy here, as in the scenes discussed from *The Idiot*, derives from the visual dimension. The narrator and the reader stand at a fixed point of observation, as if watching the action on a stage set divided in half by a closed door. The compounding of ironies depends on the reader's detachment, and, indeed, reinforces this detachment. But when he watches the insect Gregor turn the key with his toothless mouth, cracking and tearing the tissues, the scene becomes unbearable. Why? Partly because of Kafka's skill in making Gregor engage our sympathies and reflect our anxieties even in such an outlandish situation, but also because the narrator's objectivity makes his report so vivid and convincing. The comedy disarms the viewer, tricks him into opening his eyes fully to a scene that suddenly turns disgusting and intensely frightening. One moment the everyday world is destroyed with the assurance that the result is laughable; the next moment the fixed viewpoint and comic structure are maintained, but the situation's logic is carried beyond the threshold of laughter.

With the closed door dividing the set and separating Gregor the insect from the human characters, the scene is precariously balanced. If, as Martin Greenberg persuasively argues, the climax is the opening sentence, the peripety gathers all the potentialities into a kind of stasis. When the door is open the equilibrium is upset, and the story's action is impelled forward with all the melodrama and farce of an old-time movie. The chief clerk utters a loud "Oh!" clasps a hand to his mouth "as if driven by some invisible steady pressure." Gregor's mother, her hair "still undone and sticking up in all directions," clasps her hands, looks at the father, takes two steps toward Gregor, and swoons into her outspread skirts. The father knots his fist "with a fierce expression on his face as if he meant to knock Gregor back into his room," then looks around with uncertainty, and finally covers his eyes and weeps. And now we can imagine Groucho Marx playing Gregor the insect: first he takes in the scene, then he assures the human characters with perfect composure, "I'll put my clothes on at once, pack up my samples and start off."

This kind of incongruous action occurs whenever Gregor the insect confronts the human characters. We see him climb up the wall to protect his last possession—a magazine illustration of a woman wrapped in furs. We watch the father drive him into his room with apples, one of which lands and sinks into his soft back; and then we see the hysterical mother rushing toward the father in her underbodice, leaving behind a trail of loosened petticoats. We view the large insect, "covered with dust; fluff and hair and remnants of food . . . caught on his back and along his sides . . . advancing a little over the spotless floor of the living room" and ecstatically listening to his sister play the violin. All these scenes show that Gregor is helpless to change his absurd and threatening situation, and, what is worse, he cannot even put up a struggle. For the situation is such that all of his action is irrelevant; and the more farcical the scene, the more irrelevant he becomes. There is only one possibility for Gregor, and it is this possibility to which the story's logic leads—a point of total inaction, or death. In Gregor's upside-down world the only possible action is inaction; Kafka develops this contradiction in all its absurdity in "The Hunger Artist." But while inaction is a release from his death-in-life, it too is irrelevant to the process of living. Gregor Samsa, so very human within his insect shell, is an alien in the inhuman world of "The Metamorphosis," and he becomes a threat to the inhuman process of life. The nature of his threat is different from that of Joseph K. in *The Trial*. As we shall see in the next chapter, K. is an intruder, a threat from within, a man whose purposes collide with those of the inhabitants of his world; as an intruder he will have to be expelled and destroyed. But Gregor remains permanently estranged from the world he inhabits because he is encased in the shell of an insect. As a son and brother he remains unseen and unfelt; it is only as an insect that he becomes a threat to the bourgeois existence of his family. He is not expelled, he turns of his own volition and painfully crawls into his own room. He is not destroyed, he stops living. The comedy in *The Trial* works to show K. as an intruder, and it is one of the means by which the intruder is assaulted and expelled. The comedy in "The Metamorphosis" shows Gregor to be irrelevant to his world. The last reference to Gregor is made by the charwoman, her "ostrich feather standing upright on her hat" and "giggling so amicably that she could not at once continue . . . 'you don't need to bother about how to get rid of the thing next door. It's been seen to already.' "

In both Dostoyevsky and Kafka we are aware of forces beyond human control, but while we witness the effects of these forces—Myshkin is destroyed, Gregor rendered irrelevant—we never see the forces objectified or actually at work. Frederick Hoffman, in *The Mortal No*, traces the history of death from "circumstances of calculated risk or predictable consequences to the condition of the impersonal, unreasonable, unreal, and unseen assailant." In the twentieth century, according to Hoffman, we have witnessed a change in the source of violence; earlier it was a human being, then a machine, and now it is the very landscape. Hoffman's fine simile, "the assailant as landscape," explains a great deal about *The Idiot* and "The Metamorphosis," but perhaps more can be explained by focusing on the artistic strategy of these works. Our awareness of forces beyond human control comes not from the content but from the form; as Marshall McLuhan would say, the medium is the message. In both Dostoyevsky and Kafka we are startled by the sudden mechanization of a scene; narration is vividly objectified, the physical replaces the intellectual, the human voice is obliterated, characters are turned into caricatures, action becomes incongruous and follows the law of inertia. All these techniques are more common to slapstick drama, the vaudeville stage, and early films than they are to the novel. The sudden mechanization of scenes in *The Idiot* and "The Metamorphosis" are like the transformation scenes in the early movies and the English Pantomime. They destroy a comfortable and predictable pattern, they obliterate the line between man and thing, they evoke our awareness of a powerful and capricious controlling force.

If transformation is the key to the kind of terror we experience in *The Idiot* and "The Metamorphosis," the peripety, or reversal, will become the most important element in the plot. The difference between Dostoyevsky's and Kafka's worlds are in large part due to the different positions of the peripeties in their works. Myshkin has most of a long novel to struggle against his transformation; Gregor is transformed from the start. The world of *The Idiot* may be pessimistic, a Christian Fool is turned into a puppet, but there is a contest. In "The Metamorphosis" there is no struggle at all; the transformation makes Gregor irrelevant before the story begins.

3

The *Alazon*
The Theme of Intrusion in *Great Expectations* and *The Trial*

In *The Idiot* and "The Metamorphosis," our outrage and despair result from seeing humane characters gratuitously transformed into mechanical or subhuman creatures, permanently *estranged* from the human order. In *Great Expectations* and, more intensely, in *The Trial* these same emotions result from seeing humane characters *excluded* from the human order. Myshkin and Gregor are aliens, Pip and Joseph K. are intruders. These categories are not of course totally or finally delimiting, but they are designed to reveal an important distinction. The alien is a permanent outsider, unnecessary and essentially unseen and unfelt; he is estranged because of the radical difference between himself and those inside. The intruder is an outsider who has come within; he is seen and felt as a result of his collisions with those inside; he is excluded or expelled because he is a threat to the existing social and natural orders.

In all four works the world is dominated by a capricious and menacing power. In *The Idiot* and "The Metamorphosis" the power is transcendent, revealed in the formal ordering of events, the slapstick and cinematic transformations of human beings into mechanical or subhuman figures. The primary conflict in these works is between the protagonist and the unseen power, but because the power is transcendent and unseen this conflict

26

is not dramatized. The protagonist remains an alien because he is denied essential recognition by this power and hence by all those within the social and natural orders. Dostoyevsky, striving against the kind of pessimism we see full grown in Kafka, tempers his story with the inclusion of Mme Epanchin.

In *Great Expectations* and *The Trial*, the power is an energy that inheres in the environment; Hoffman's view of "the assailant as landscape" is pertinent to these works, and his essay on *The Trial* is one of the most revealing we have. In these works the primary conflict is between the protagonist and the landscape, or the irrational and inherent energy that activates it. Here the conflict is dramatized, however bewilderingly, and while the protagonist may never be recognized for himself, he is given recognition as an intruder.

The archetypal intruder was the *alazon* or impostor of classical comedy. While Oedipus is an impostor and an intruder, these elements are not emphasized as they are in comedy: his definition as a hero overrides the fact that he is an impostor; his arousal of fear is a result of his being seen as an integral part of the social and natural order, not as an intruder from outside. The *alazon* belongs to the comic ritual, where, as Francis Cornford shows, his pretensions are exposed, and his intrusion into the natural and social order is dealt with by verbal and physical assaults leading to his final expulsion. There are major and minor *alazons*, who play different kinds of roles in Old and New Comedy, but my main point can be made by examining Aristophanes' paradigmatic *Clouds*.

Strepsiades tries to subvert the social order when, in hope of outwitting his creditors, he sends his son, Pheidippides, to Socrates' Thoughtery. By doing so he aligns himself with the forces of not only social but cosmic disorder: it is important that, after Socrates invokes the

Clouds and expounds on their nature, he proves that they are the only gods—that Zeus does not exist, and that Vortex is king. Playing with Anaxagoras's idea that God transformed chaos into order by means of Vortex, Aristophanes shows Vortex as the vacuum, the negative energy from which chaos derives. Strepsiades' acceptance of Socrates' view is the turning point of the play, which was foreshadowed in the *agon* of Right Logic and Wrong Logic. The result is the destruction of logical, social, and natural order, and the creation of a world where verbal and physical collision is the law. Pheidippides beats his father and proves to him that it is right for a son to beat his father; he is just about to prove the justice of beating one's mother. This is the second *agon* in the play, and the point of maximum chaos. Strepsiades is comically exposed as an impostor and as an intruder, and is expelled from his own victory feast. He brings the play to a close by restoring order in his renunciation of Vortex, his acceptance of Zeus, and his comic destruction of Socrates' Thoughtery. When Socrates asks him what he is doing on the roof, Strepsiades answers with an irony that turns Socrates' upside-down argument aright: "I walk on air, and contemplate the Sun."

Great Expectations and *The Trial* are similar to *The Clouds* in form but opposite in essence. In the worlds of Dickens and Kafka the laws of life and of society, while inevitable and necessary, drive everyone and everything to act at cross purposes, to continually collide physically and psychologically. As a result, the character who appears most humane, because he is self-conscious, sees himself—and hence defines himself—as an intruder. In his essay "Aminadab or the Fantastic Considered as a Language" Sartre carries Dostoyevsky's conception of "the fantastic" to an extreme; he describes the laws, which could be better termed the activating energy, of this kind of world as "a revolt of means against ends."

When I enter a café, the first thing I perceive are implements. Not things, not raw matter, but utensils: tables, seats, mirrors, glasses and saucers. Each of these represents a piece of domesticated matter. Taken as a whole, they belong to an obvious order. The meaning of this ordering is an *end*—an end that is myself, or rather, the man in me, the consumer that I am. Such is the surface appearance of the human world. It would be useless for us to look for "raw material" in this world. Here the means functions as matter, and form —mental order—is represented by the end. Now let us describe the café topsy-turvy.

We will have to show ends crushed by their own means and trying vainly to pierce the enormous layers of matter or, if you prefer, objects that reveal their own instrumentality, but with an indiscipline and disorderly power, a kind of coarse independence that suddenly snatches their end from us just when we think we have it fast. Here, for example, is a door. It is there before us, with its hinges, latch and lock. It is carefully bolted, as if protecting some treasure. I manage, after several attempts, to procure a key; I open it, only to find that behind it is a wall. I sit down and order a cup of coffee. The waiter makes me repeat the order three times and repeats it himself to avoid any possibility of error. He dashes off and repeats my order to a second waiter, who notes it down in a little book and transmits it to a third waiter. Finally, a fourth waiter comes back and, putting an inkwell on my table, says, "There you are." "But," I say, "I ordered a cup of coffee." "That's right," he says, as he walks off.

If the reader, while reading a story of this kind, thinks that the waiters are playing a joke or that they are involved in some collective psychosis, then we have lost the game. But if we have been able to give him the impression that we are talking about a world in which these absurd manifestations appear as normal behavior, then he will find himself plunged all at once into the heart of the fantastic. The fantastic is the revolt of means against ends; either the object in question noisily asserts itself as a means, concealing its end through the very violence of its assertion, or it refers back to another means, and this one to still another, and so on *ad infinitum*, without our ever being able to discover the ultimate end, or else some interference in means belonging to independent series gives us a glimpse of a composite and blurred image of contradictory ends.

In *Great Expectations* and *The Trial*, objects and people are turned into instruments, impelled by a capricious energy to act against the ends for which they would appear to be designed. Rebellion of means against ends is the basis of social and natural processes. The protagonist is a threat to these processes because, being self-conscious, he defines himself as a creature with a distinct end. Every natural, human action or reaction leads him to see himself, and the reader to see him, as an intruder in the natural and human world. The anxiety aroused in both the protagonist and the reader is due to a fear of more than unjust punishment or destruction, but of life itself—and this, Wolfgang Kayser points out, is what distinguishes the Grotesque from other forms of art.

Dickens evokes just such a fear of life in his introduction of Pip in the opening pages of *Great Expectations*.

My first most vivid and broad impression of the identity of things, seems to me to have been gained on a memorable raw afternoon towards evening. At such a time I found out for certain, that this bleak place overgrown with nettles was the churchyard; and that Philip Pirrip, late of this parish, and also Georgiana wife of the above, were dead and buried; and that Alexander, Bartholomew, Abraham, Tobias, and Roger, infant children of the aforesaid, were also dead and buried; and that the dark flat wilderness beyond the churchyard, intersected with dykes and mounds and gates, with scattered cattle feeding on it, was the marshes; and that the low leaden line beyond was the river; and that the distant savage lair from which the wind was rushing, was the sea; and that the small bundle of shivers growing afraid of it all and beginning to cry, was Pip.

In Pip's world there is an obscure identity between the objects of nature and the dead members of his family; both are inscrutable, uncontrollable, and mysteriously threatening. And it is important to note that Pip locates himself, "the small bundle of shivers," as a part of the menacing scene.

Pip "found out for certain" his identity in an experience that permanently excluded him from the physical world, excluded him even from the self he saw and felt to be inhabiting this world. The experience was signaled by a terrible voice coming from among the graves, "Hold your noise. . . . Keep still, you little devil, or I'll cut your throat." The fearful man in the leg iron "had been soaked in water, and smothered in mud, and lamed by stones, and cut by flints, and stung by nettles, and torn by briars"; in short he had been aggressively afflicted by the objects of the same marsh that was identified with Pip's dead family, and that defined Pip as "the small bundle of shivers." The natural objects, dark animals, dead relations, and escaped convict compose a world that includes the shivering Pip. Yet they all seem to be driven by a mysterious, contradictory, and aggressive energy that turns him into an intruder. Pip sees himself at once as a part of this world and as an intruder in it; hence the anxiety that pervades the novel, and hence the continuing two-dimensional point of view.

The narrator of *Great Expectations* tells the story from the vantage of a mature man looking back with humane judgment at his initiation into life, but he conveys the emotional responses from the viewpoint of the evolving protagonist. In his book on *Dickens and Kafka*, Mark Spilka makes the interesting observation that both writers see the world from the perspective of their arrested childhood, and that such a perspective, being close to the animalistic and "below the sight-line of adult activity," ideally accommodates the traits of the

Grotesque. What Spilka obscures in his sensitive psychological reading is that in the tone of Dickens's narrative there is a note of tolerant amusement. Sometimes soft, sometimes strong, this note derives from the two-dimensional point of view. The simultaneous perspectives cause us to feel the boy's terror and laugh at his situation at the same time. We might remember that *The Idiot* and "The Metamorphosis" contain instances of simultaneous perspective. While the laughter in Dickens does not effect the same derangement as Dostoyevsky's or Kafka's, since it often leads into strains of sentimentality, in the best scenes it heightens the sense of contradictoriness and irrationality, and, as in classical comedy, enforces our view of Pip as an intruder or *alazon*.

There are two scenes which show Pip as an intruder, and which help us see more clearly the role comedy plays in the novel. The first is where Pip takes Joe Gargery to Miss Havisham's. When Estella opens the gate, Joe takes off his hat and stands "weighing it by the brim in both hands: as if he had some urgent reason in his mind for being particular to half a quarter of an ounce." When he is led into the presence of Miss Havisham, sitting at her dressing table, bedecked in white satin and sparkling jewels, he stands like "some extraordinary bird . . . with his tuft of feathers ruffled, and his mouth open as if he wanted a worm." And when Miss Havisham addresses him formally, "You are the husband . . . of the sister of this boy?" Joe answers "in a manner that was at once expressive of forcible argumentation, strict confidence, and great politeness"—but directing his answer to Pip instead of Miss Havisham: "Which I meantersay, Pip . . . as I hup and married your sister, and I were at the time what you might call (if you was any ways inclined) a single man."

In his sister's house, which is also identified with the dark forces of the graveyard and the marshes, Pip has been made to feel like an intruder in every one of his natural actions. This has been the normal world for Pip, the world of everyday from which Miss Havisham's house is an escape. But just because of her house's total unfamiliarity—its great dismal appearance, the fantastic presence of its mistress, the contradictory behavior of Estella, and such surprises as a delicate young man springing out of the cucumber frames to engage him in a fistfight—Pip is made to feel even more of an intruder here. The one source of security to Pip is Joe, his uncle and his soul mate, and when Joe is brought into Miss Havisham's world and Pip is forced to see him as a totally ridiculous figure, this security is destroyed. Joe fights against it comically by addressing the answers to Miss Havisham's questions directly to Pip, but the struggle only serves to make Joe as strange as Miss Havisham and Estella. Miss Havisham and Joe frantically asserting themselves for obscure purposes are pictured as capricious instruments, or in Sartre's words, means fantastically rebelling against ends. This scene at Miss Havisham's complements the scene with Magwitch at the graveyard: both identify the natural and the unnatural; both connect with Pip's early home life; both hold out the promise and/or threat of an unnatural surrogate parent. In short, both together give Pip a full sense of his identity as an intruder in a strange world.

Further, the scene that begins with Joe weighing his hat "as if he had some urgent reason in his mind for being particular to half a quarter of an ounce" ends with Joe exchanging Pip's indentures for a bag of coins, and leads to the scene where Pip is legally bound over in a way that created "the general impression in Court that I had been taken red-handed." Just as the early scene with Magwitch gave Pip's undefined guilt a legal dimension, the scene at Miss Havisham's makes Pip aware that his purposes are somehow at odds with those of the law—

that he is an intruder not only in the natural world but in the social world as well. By the end of the next chapter Pip's exclusion is complete: "I remember that when I got into my little bedroom, I was truly wretched, and had a strong conviction on me that I should never like Joe's trade. I had liked it once, but once was not now." Within the next few pages we are introduced to the figure who replaces Pip in Joe's world, the dark and menacing Orlick, and before the end of the novel we come to see Pip as an intruder in the very world he once felt as his only security.

The second comic scene is at Wemmick's Castle, the one refuge from the materialistic and legalistic world of London. The Sunday tea contrasts markedly with the early Sunday teas in the home of Pip's sister and with the recent dinner at Lawyer Jaggers. All "warm and greasy" after the meal, they sit around the fire and listen to Aged Parent read the newspaper. Wemmick and Miss Skiffins sit side by side, and Pip from his shadowy corner observes "a slow and gradual elongation of Mr. Wemmick's mouth, powerfully suggestive of his slowly and gradually stealing his arm round Miss Skiffins's waist." Before long he sees Wemmick's hand appear on the other side of Miss Skiffins, "but at that same moment Miss Skiffins neatly stopped him with the green glove, unwound his arm again as if it were an article of dress, and with the greatest deliberation laid it on the table before her."

The Castle is an oasis. Wemmick has created a world secure from the threats of London, through sheer whimsicality. In London people are turned into mechanical instruments serving no collective or visible end by an immanent energy. In the Castle these instruments are turned back into humane people because, like the many mechanical contrivances in the Castle, they serve no end other than an innocent and natural delight. Yet we are gradually made aware that the energy activating the people of London and the natural desires of those in the Castle are related. The moat separating the two worlds is only an arm's length wide. When Wemmick's natural desires are aroused, he and Miss Skiffins become figures of an animated cartoon.

We come to understand, as we comprehend the relationship between the worlds of London and the Castle, that the orders of Nature and Law are ultimately one. The action is no less comic and no less mechanical when after their marriage "Mrs. Wemmick no longer unwound Wemmick's arm when it adapted itself to her figure, but sat in a highbacked chair against the wall, like a violincello in its case, and submitted to being embraced as that melodious instrument might have done." Whether malign or benign, all the characters in *Great Expectations* are energized to act mechanically and, hence, counter to human purposes—they are comically revealed as instruments, or means rebelling against ends.

Miss Havisham's house and Wemmick's Castle appear to be polar opposites. Each a retreat from the world of London, one is into the dark world of dreams, the other into the light world of fancy. But neither proves to be a real escape; in fact, both reveal the world of everyday in surprising depth. Furthermore, they both hold out promises to Pip that are unattainable: wealth and family security. The promises are unattainable because Pip is no more at home in Miss Havisham's dressing room than he is, sitting in his shadowy corner, in the Castle. As promises they entangle Pip in the world of the novel; as taunts they exclude him from this world.

In the scenes just discussed, Pip's entanglement and exclusion are developed through comic action; we can also look beyond the action to see how Dickens developed the texture of his fantastic world. The tone of the entire narrative underscores the complexity, the two strains of the narrative voice simultaneously accenting the involvement with sympathy and the exclusion with humane detachment. However it is at deeper levels that Dickens's world of the fantastic is fully revealed, and Dorothy Van Ghent has made what would be an excellent case for Sartre's thesis. First, she points to the number of conversations where each participant "raptly" soliloquizes in a "fantastic private language." Joe Gargery's language is the most obviously fantastic, especially in his confrontations with Miss Havisham and Lawyer Jaggers, but there is also Miss Havisham's formal parlance and Jaggers' legal jargon, Mrs. Joe's irrelevant and repetitious "Be grateful to them which brought you up by hand," and Mr. Pumblechook's "May I?—May I?" Second, Mrs. Van Ghent discusses the animation of objects: "A four-poster bed in an inn, where Pip goes to spend the night, is a despotic monster that straddles over the whole room, 'putting one of his arbitrary legs into the fireplace, and another into the doorway, and squeezing the wretched little washing-stand in quite a Divinely Righteous manner.' Houses, looking down through the skylight of Jaggers' office in London, twist themselves in order to spy on Pip like police agents . . . a meek little muffin has to be 'confined with the utmost precaution under a strong iron cover,' and a hat set on a mantlepiece, demands constant attention . . . but its ingenuity is such that it finally manages to fall into the slop basin." Third, Mrs. Van Ghent focuses on the way Dickens isolates parts of the body: Jaggers' huge forefinger, Wemmick's "post-office mouth," Magwitch's clicking throat—all seem to be obeying capricious and inscrutable laws. Finally, she defines the essential quality of this world by pointing out the shock and collision of "human fragments": Magwitch surprises Pip at the graveyard, soldiers extending handcuffs block Pip as he flees from the table, Miss Havisham points her finger and commands Pip to play, a young gentleman springs out of the cucumber frames to butt Pip in the stomach.

Through the breakdown of language, Mrs. Van Ghent explains, Dickens begins to convey the breakdown of order. Through the vitalization of objects and the isolation of human parts Dickens composes "a world of dissociated and apparently lawless fragments"; he also evokes the "quaint gaiety of a forbidden life and an aggressiveness that has got out of control." But by underscoring Mrs. Van Ghent's point about shocks and collisions we can carry her conclusions even further. More than a breakdown of order, the breakdown of language suggests the endless oppositions of innumerable orders. More than lawless, the human and nonhuman fragments seem to be driven by separate and eccentric laws. More than aggressing, these fragments seem to be colliding.

The distinctive comedy in *Great Expectations* is the result of the multitude of collisions. The major collisions shock Pip into realizing that he is an intruder. The pervasiveness of collisions—characters battering each other with their private languages, objects senselessly asserting themselves against each other, parts of bodies assaulting one another—create the real anxiety. The distinctive terror in *Great Expectations* comes from the discovery that the world in which Pip finds himself an intruder is not homogeneous, that the forces directed against him are infinite and infinitely different.

Dickens did not sustain his comic terror to the extent of any of the more modern writers I am discussing, probably because he was much more optimistic about the possibilities for social progress. Yet what makes *Great Expectations* far more than a piece of social satire is that he so thoroughly interrelated the social and natural orders, showing them both to be parts of the same capricious and heterogeneous process. There is no way of telling whether Pip's nightmare is reality or his response to reality, whether it is the result of an unjust and menacing social system or whether the social system is unjust and menacing because of natural human drives. Miss Havisham, the weird goddess figure who proves not to be a goddess; Magwitch, the figure of natural and social menace who turns out to embody Fortune; Orlick, the figure of irrational evil, brought to life, as it were, by the accident of Pip's continuing good fortune; and Joe, the figure of unreasoning goodness—all collide with Pip as members of society, but they are also projections of Pip's natural desires and possibilities. Some of the most important collisions in the novel externalize conflicting inner drives, and these are related to collisions in the outer reality of Society and Nature. Pip is so entangled in and excluded from such a thoroughly chaotic world that there is no basis for distinguishing between the psychological and the physical, the individual and the social. The two-dimensional point of view is not just the conjunction of youth and age, but of perspectives that are simultaneously rebellious and adjustive. Although the story moves toward the adjustive, a deep sense of the reality he created kept Dickens at first from writing a happy ending. And even in the revised ending, written as a concession to popular taste, there is a strain of ambivalence based on the impossibility of harmony or final adjustment in the world of *Great Expectations*.

Also simultaneously entangled in and excluded from the world is Joseph K. of Kafka's *Trial*. In the opening paragraph of the novel, as Frederick Hoffman points out, the normal life of the hero is unexpectedly interrupted, signaling the "intrusion of the absurd into a world protected on all sides by familiar assurances and securities."

Someone must have traduced Joseph K., for without having done anything wrong he was arrested one fine morning. His landlady's cook, who always brought him his breakfast at eight o'clock, failed to appear on this occasion. That had never happened before. K. waited for a little while longer, watching from his pillow the old lady opposite who seemed to be peering at him with a curiosity unusual even for her, but then, feeling both put out and hungry, he rang the bell. At once there was a knock at the door and a man entered whom he had never seen before in the house. He was slim and yet well knit, he wore a closely fitting black suit, which was furnished with all sorts of pleats, pockets, buckles, and buttons, as well as a belt, like a tourist's outfit, and in consequence looked eminently practical, though one could not quite tell what actual purpose it served.

From K.'s point of view this is indeed an intrusion, and much that follows supports his view. The warders have brought his subordinates from the bank right into his home; they take over the room of his neighbor, Fräulein Bürstner; they intrude menacingly into his mind, since "with these people beside him he could not even think"; and they intrude physically in a manner that turns the scene into a farce, "the belly of the second warder . . . butting against him in an almost friendly way." Yet, due to the objective third person narration, we get more than K.'s viewpoint, and we are led to draw more complex and ambiguous conclusions. The neighbor lady peers at K. as if *he* were somehow out of place. When his natural impatience and appetite require, *he* rings the bell, breaking the silence and equilibrium, and seeming to bring on the knock of the arresting officer. The officer, an efficient looking man wearing a suit designed for a practical purpose totally irrelevant to anything K. can imagine, implies to K. that his request for breakfast is out of order. All of K.'s natural reactions, physical and psychological, seem to be at cross purposes with the order of life, which is established in the first sentence of the novel and asserts itself to the very end.

With the intrusion of the warders, agents of the Law, the absurd, or more accurately the fantastic, is identified with the social order; and we soon come to see that it is identified with the natural order as well. The first chapter follows K. through the course of a single day—just as the novel follows K. through the course of a single year—from sleep to sleep. The day starts with a mysterious menace to the physical and psychological life of Joseph K. But ironically K. begins rising from a state of physical and psychological inertness, symbolic of his life before the intrusion, and he ends in a high moment of vitality, seizing Fräulein Bürstner, and kissing her "first on the lips, then all over the face, like some thirsty animal lapping greedily at a spring of long-sought fresh water." In the beginning of the chapter he is intruded upon by agents of the order of life. By the end of the chapter, vitalized by the surprise of his arrest, he intrudes himself into Fräulein Bürstner's room and life. His confession to her of what happened that morning leads her to define him as an intruder then as well as now. His desire to right the wrong, to fight against the intruding order, turns him into its ridiculous and purposeless instrument; and this is dramatized in his comic reenactment of the arrest for Fräulein Bürstner.

Frederick Hoffman makes the point that every form of violence includes an assailant and a victim, and that there is an implicit or formal "collaboration" between the two since "the assailant strikes with force" and "the victim receives the force." When the distance between the assailant and victim increases to such an extent as to preclude "moral and emotional visibility," essential changes in the relationship occur. The scene of violence, or the landscape, being the only evidence for motive, assumes the role of assailant. This means that every object and every person in the normal scene becomes a menace, and surprise becomes an essential element in the violence. Further, since the scene includes the victim, he too becomes identified with the assailant. *The Trial* is composed of a series of scenes in which K.

searches energetically and futilely for his assailant; and his very search becomes a source of violence. The condition of the world is such that the victim is forced to become the assailant to others and to himself.

Hoffman realizes in great intellectual and emotional depth what we might call the tragic dimension of the novel. I would like to complement his study by focusing on the comic elements, for surprise, one of the most important elements in Hoffman's analysis, belongs not so much to tragedy (the emphasis of recognition is opposed to that of surprise) as to comedy. The surprise, the incongruence, the caricature, the pantomime of the first chapter are all essentially comic devices that work to enforce the theme of intrusion. In the next chapter, K.'s search for the Court is formally comic; he intrudes into an alien neighborhood, invents a joiner named Lanz to disguise his true purpose, hears his query passed from tenant to tenant in the crowded apartment. In the courtroom, so crowded that many people are compelled to "stand only in a bent posture with their heads and backs knocking against the ceiling," K. is equally absurd as an intruder and as a man intruded upon. The swarming crowd seems to have gathered for its own purposes; "a fat little wheezing man who was talking with much merriment to a man sprawling just behind him . . . flung his arms into the air, as if he were caricaturing someone. The lad who was escorting K. found it difficult to announce his presence. Twice he stood on tiptoe and tried to say something, without being noticed by the man up above. Not till one of the people on the platform pointed out the lad did the man turn to him and bend down to hear his faltered words. Then he drew out his watch and with a quick glance at K., 'You should have been here an hour and five minutes ago.'" K. is crushed against the table and forced to brace himself in order to keep from knocking the Examining Magistrate off the platform. He is mistaken for a house painter. His commonplace remarks are received with enthusiastic applause and derisive laughter by opposing factions, while his moral argument is interrupted by the rape of a washerwoman.

The comedy in *The Trial* is very much like that in *Great Expectations*, the result of collisions; in a world as crowded as a Bosch painting everyone is forced to intrude on everyone else's privacy. All private and public relations are affected. What distinguishes the private relationships in the seduction scenes is not, as some critics have suggested, K.'s selfish purposes. He may have finally turned the washerwoman and Leni into (ineffective) instruments to achieve the end of his acquittal; but the scenes derive their dark erotic attraction largely from the playfully irrelevant discoveries and the surprising intrusions. K. begins with feelings of irritation when, after showing him the Examining Magistrate's pornographic ledgers, the washerwoman seats herself next to him and looks into his "lovely dark eyes." And he is drawn away from his initial purpose, a matter of life and death—until Bertold, the student, intrudes, lifts her in one arm and carries her up the staircase, "very slowly, puffing and groaning," while the washerwoman waves to K. and shrugs her shoulders "to suggest that she was not to blame for this abduction." Later, K. seeks out Leni when his best interests would be served by attending to her employer, the Lawyer Huld, and Leni seduces him by calling attention to her grotesquely webbed hand. Afterward, completely distracted by his thoughts of Leni, he fails to notice his uncle, until the man "seized him by the arms and banged him against the house door as if he wanted to nail him there," and railed at Joseph for leaving him, the sick lawyer, and the Chief Clerk of the Court to sit "for minutes on end in complete silence, listening for you to come back."

Public relationships are initiated by the intrusion of

the Law into K.'s life. Lawyers become necessary, although even they are irrelevant since they are excluded by law from their client's proceedings; but they are nevertheless continually intruding and being intruded upon. And throughout the novel their dignity is comically assailed. Huld is pictured in his sickbed, blinded by the candlelight, being caressed by a bright young maid with a doll-like face and a webbed hand. Among the anterooms of the Court we watch a lawyer climb on his colleague's back to peer out of the skylight; and we see one lawyer after another rushing up the stairs and being hurled back down, as they attempt to tire out an aged attendant. When after great psychological and physical exertion K. discovers the painter Titorelli, who understands the workings of the Law, he is forced to listen to a complicated discourse on the alternatives of ostensible acquittal or postponement in an overheated room, which is crammed full of paintings and furniture, and into which the snickers and gibes of deformed, degenerate, and leering teenage girls continually obtrude. And he is forced to escape the harpies by climbing over a feather bed, burdened with a pile of identical heathscapes which the artist has intimidated him into buying.

Warders intrude into K.'s bedroom; courtrooms and law offices appear in ordinary apartment buildings. Administrators of justice invade K.'s place of business, compelling him to intrude upon a private whipping scene. But as we are continually reminded, there is no separation of the public and the private, and every victim of intrusion is at the same time an intruder. K. has been responsible for the whipping of his warders; he invaded their normal routine when, in the name of justice, he complained about them in Court. That justice is carried out in this case is indeed a surprise, as is the comic exposure of fat Willem, who gained his size by eating the breakfasts of suspects, and Franz, who tries to escape his punishment by inventing the tale of a waiting sweet-heart. This scene of multiple intrusions, shocks, and collisions, is like all the others I have described in that it gathers its menace from the intimation of a ubiquitous and immanent power of judgment and execution, and from the incongruence of a menacing situation and comic characterization or action. The surprises, intrusions, overcrowdings, collisions, assaults are psychologically threatening to Joseph K. With the emphasis, indeed exaggeration, of the physical, they serve as comic devices to show K. as irrelevant to the natural order of life and continually in the way of all human beings. To be irrelevant and in the way is how Sartre, in his early existentialist phase, described the human condition; an awareness of this condition aroused feelings of physical disgust (hence the title of his first novel, *Nausea*), which could be overcome by stoic acceptance and anguished, and in a sense heroic, choice. To Kafka an awareness of his condition allows man no such choice; rather it serves to reveal man's psychological and physical exclusion. It does not show man as an alien but as an impostor in his human pretensions and as an intruder in the normal world.

The Trial, like *Great Expectations*, follows the paradigmatic pattern of Aristophanes' *Clouds*: the *alazon*, aligned with the forces of disorder, or ultimately Vortex, is exposed, assaulted, and expelled. But because we are drawn into the worlds of Kafka and, to a lesser extent, Dickens, and because Vortex is not an aberration but the law of nature and society, the ultimate result is not comic. In the opening scene of each novel the protagonist is intruded upon by the forces of law and life. The acceptance of these forces is a recognition of existential guilt. This is not the guilt of original sin; it derives from a feeling that man is a permanent intruder in his own world. Paradoxically, both novels move from death to

life. In *Great Expectations* the movement is clear and
explicit, and while it does not finally ameliorate the
menace in Dickens's fantastic world, it does reflect Dickens's basic optimism. In *The Trial* the movement is only
formal, working ironically against the inexorable process
of destruction; hence the far greater degree of pessimism.
There are sufficient hints in *The Trial* to suggest that
Joseph K.'s previous existence, selfish and bourgeois, was
a living death. When he resists the intruders, it is the
result of an awakened moral sensitivity. He is brought to
life morally as well as physically; and yet each act of
resistance makes him an accomplice of the Law. His
resistance gives him a new and surprising vitality. This is
dramatized in the end of the first chapter when he hungrily kisses Fräulein Bürstner, and in his erotic relations
with the other women in the novel; it is also demon-
strated in his passionate and selfless plea in Court, and in
his lonely, stubborn, and senseless pursuance of his case.
But he is brought to life as an intruder; he is shown to be
an accomplice not only of the Law, which threatens him,
but of the Forces of Life, which will finally destroy him.

The *agon* in *The Trial* is between Right Logic and
Wrong Logic, between Order and Vortex, but the normal relationship is reversed. We might say that this is a
comic treatment of the comic ritual. Joseph K., awakened to an awareness that human life should be an end
and not a means, becomes an intruder in a world where
Vortex, or rebellion of means against ends, is the law. In
the priest's sermon, man is compelled to enter a door
designed exclusively for him; he is no alien. But the door
will never be opened to him. Man is simultaneously
singled out and excluded, called into being as a means
rather than as an end, and denied the possibility of
achieving the end for which the means was designed.
The novel is composed of a series of scenes which are
formally comic, which show that Vortex not logic or

human purpose is the basis of existence, and which turn Joseph K. into an instrument and finally into an animal. His final expulsion is a restoration not of order but of chaos. The comedy of *The Trial* turned against itself does not evoke a joy of living but a fear of life.

4

Faulkner's One Ring Circus
Light in August

In *Light in August* William Faulkner also turns comedy against itself to build a world that is almost as terrifying as Kafka's, and he shows Joe Christmas to be as much a tragic *alazon* as Joseph K. But Faulkner's view of life was fundamentally comic, and the form that enabled him to express total irrationality and outrageous violence also offered him possibilities that were redemptive.

Although *Light in August* deals with the most serious social problems and describes a world that is profoundly grim, it derives its singular energy from caricature and farce. Think of Byron Bunch, whom you wouldn't see if "he was alone by himself in the bottom of a empty concrete swimming pool," and then picture him as he walks toward the truck "like he had eggs under his feet" and ineptly tries to climb into bed with Lena. Lucas Brown is likened to a running car with a loud radio and no driver; when he is locked in the room with Lena, who has just become the mother of his baby, he tiptoes past her and, with hasty assurances, bounds through the rear window. Lena on the road to Jefferson thinks with serene pride, "Like a lady I et," and then dips her fingers into a can of oily sardines. Not a single character in the novel escapes Faulkner's comic eye, and while these characters and scenes are almost purely comic, many that are not at all funny are nonetheless formed by the same kind of mold. There are the comic-strip flashes of Bobbie Allen, a prostitute in the shape of a child, with eyes "like the button eyes of a toy animal"; and of her employer, Max, with a broad hat always slanted on his head and a cigarette always burning in the corner of his mouth. The Reverend Hightower wildly preaches sermons about a grandfather who, moments after daring to burn a well-stocked enemy warehouse, is killed by a woman as he tries to steal a chicken. McEachern, with his nightshirt thrust into his trousers and braces dangling, dismounts from a white horse and charges into a dance hall in search of a prodigal foster son. Young Christmas hides in a closet and slowly devours a tube of toothpaste while a dietician and intern make love. Joanna Burden is found dead in an attitude that symbolizes her life: her body facing one way and her head "turned clean around like she was looking behind her." Hines preaches white supremacy in a Negro church and, like a woundup doll, beats frail fists against a captive grandson, shouting, "Kill the bastard. . . . Kill him." Percy Grimm reacts with the efficiency of a well-oiled revolver at the signal of Christmas's escape, and at the same time gives the irrelevant order to turn in the fire alarm.

All these descriptions and situations are ludicrous even if they do not arouse laughter. As a matter of fact we are even more aware of the ludicrous elements—exaggeration, incongruity, absurdity—as they are less laughable. The reason for this may be that we are surprised to see characters whom the author seems to be treating seriously suddenly turn into caricatures, just as we are shocked to see frightening situations turn into farce. Bergson explains that surprise is an important element in comedy, for it is often necessary to turn the comic *de facto* into comic *de jure*, to destroy what has become a habitual perception of the customary. We might go on to say that the more habitual the perception—and the response—the more necessary the surprise; the more deeply ingrained the customary, the more profound the comedy. Faulkner shows us a world to which even the liberal humanitarian has developed a blindness, perhaps out of necessity; he shocks us into seeing this world afresh and denies us the security of a prefabricated response.

Although Bergson's view of comedy is limited, we have seen that he does explore the kind of comic structures found in the works of Dickens, Dostoyevsky, and Kafka. It is in Faulkner's *Light in August*, however, where Bergson's thesis becomes most illuminating; therefore let us review his main point. According to Bergson, we laugh when we see a running man suddenly trip over a stone, or when a man finds himself sitting on the floor after his chair is pulled from beneath him, or when a rich man acts like a miser, for the same reason—in each case the laughable element is a "mechanical inelasticity." What distinguishes man is his flexibility, his ability to adapt to changing situations. When he is suddenly seen to be rigid, to act oblivious to his surroundings out of sheer momentum, to appear like a puppet or a machine, he is ridiculous. Comedy is the presentation of something mechanical encrusted on the living. Its value lies in its rejection of the deadening effects of mechanization, in its implicit affirmation of the vital force within man. Byron, Brown, Bobbie Allen, Max, Joanna, Hightower, Hines, Grimm, even Christmas and Lena are essentially ludicrous when they appear to be puppets or machines. Yet, as in the case of the writers discussed above, we are not satisfied that Faulkner's situations are wholly funny or that his characters are totally ridiculous. If his characters act mechanically, they also have a remarkable vitality. And it is just this balance that gives Faulkner's characters their unique quality—they derive from a terrific energy struggling against a mechanical form. They are in fact the reverse of Bergson's comic types, for Faulkner brings to life the human force within the mechanical.

Through this kind of characterization Faulkner demonstrates his optimism far more convincingly than through the kind of rhetoric that culminated in his Nobel Prize speech. And the strength of his positive claim for the human spirit can be fully appreciated when we view the totally hopeless situation of his characters. Faulkner pictures his world as a puppet stage, and finally as a chess game, governed by a blind mechanism. It is this mechanism that puts the stones in the paths and pulls out the chairs; and the vital energy of the characters only contributes to the machine's dynamic. In such a world, characters are turned into caricatures, and the only form that action can take is tragic farce.

Light in August dramatizes the predicament of modern man, who is denied his individual form of vital energy—his identity—because society offers only rigid, mechanical, legalistic, and essentially irrelevant categories for identification: race, religion, sex. The color symbolism is more than just a brilliant artistic device to connect these categories. Black and white accentuate the either/or nature of their demands; for there is no compromise between being Negro or white, "Christian" or immoral, heterosexual or homosexual. When, as we shall see, Faulkner shows these categories to be determined not by society but by a law of the absolute, he sets the stage for his grotesque game.

The world of the grotesque is tellingly described in Jan Kott's *Shakespeare Our Contemporary*, and although Mr. Kott is discussing *Lear* and *Endgame*, his remarks are also pertinent to *Light in August*. Kott shows that in the classic tragic situation the hero is offered a choice between two exclusive alternatives, acceptance or rejection of the absolute; he suffers because his individual affirmation necessitates choosing rejection. "The tragic situation becomes grotesque when both alternatives of the choice imposed are absurd, irrelevant or compromising. The hero has to play, even if there is no game. Every move is bad, but he cannot throw down his cards." Antigone can choose between civil and divine decrees; Creon can choose to punish Antigone for disobeying his law or set her free for obeying the law of the gods. But Christmas is not offered this kind of choice. The mutually exclusive alternatives exist, and so does the compulsion for him to choose; but not only are the choices irrelevant—he is denied the opportunity to choose either. The absolute in Faulkner's world is like the practical joker who demands that his guest choose one chair or another and is prepared to pull out either one as his guest sits down.

Faulkner expresses his view of the world in the structure of his novel, which is at once naturalistic and comic. The naturalism is thorough, for Christmas is shown to be determined by his heredity and environment, and the path of his life is as inescapable as the road or corridor he continually inhabits. It is in the corridor of the orphanage that we get our first glimpse of Christmas, who looks like a small shadow in the quiet afternoon; and this is the corridor over which his grandfather Hines presides in his uncanny way, making Christmas seem different from the other boys. And when Christmas sets out on his own after striking down McEachern, his foster father, his life becomes one long street, "with imperceptible corners and changes of scene." His sexual relationship with Joanna is described "as though he had fallen into a sewer [which] . . . ran only by night." The sewer becomes the "savage and lonely street which he had chosen of his own will," for this is his first and last engagement with another human being, and the choice is a negation rather than an affirmation, which turns his street straight back to the town where he was born, and where he finally gives himself up.

Nevertheless, the novel is not completely naturalistic. What precludes naturalism is the enigma of Christmas's heredity. That we do not know whether Christmas's father was a Negro is part of the outrageous joke of the novel, and that we do know that his father was a circus man underscores the grim humor. Further, while the long central section of the novel (chapters 6–19) are perfectly chronological and follow an inexorable logic, the initial impression of the novel is not one of order but disorder, not logic but confusion. The sense of confusion is the result of mistaken identities, mechanical repetition, and geometrical complications—important comic devices and especially relevant to the Bergsonian view of comedy. Conceived on a perfectly geometrical basis, the underlying structure of the novel is partly comic. The corridors and streets along which Christmas is kept running help form the grid or stage for the novel's tragic comedy. By placing vital characters on such a stage, the author shows how they inevitably become puppets or fools, and he evokes either—and sometimes both—our pity and laughter.

The difficulty in distinguishing fathers from grandfathers in the Burden and Hightower genealogies is due to a calculated confusion of identities; Burdens alternate between Calvin and Nathaniel, Hightowers between "the father" and "the son." And the confusion of generations is amplified as we discover the resemblance between the two families: ministers ride out to the back hills to preach Sunday sermons, fathers read the Bible to sons with harsh mystical fervor, sons repudiate fathers and religion, rebellion involves sex and guilt, and the guilt of sex is transmuted into the dark sin of religion and is personified in the Negro. Joanna's grandfather and Hightower's father were both religious abolitionists and both killed a man over the Negro question. Finally the ridiculous death of Gail Hightower in a chicken coop and the senseless murder of two Calvin Burdens at a voting poll become fixations for Hightower and Joanna, who are born a generation later. The history of the Burdens and the Hightowers is a history of extremes—of commitment to and repudiation of religion; of racial strife; of sexual union between Northerners and Southerners, light and dark. The extremes and the pharisaic legalism turn the confusion into a mechanical repetitiveness and the characters into caricatures.

Another reason for our confusion with the Burdens and Hightowers is their strong resemblance to other characters, notably McEachern, Hines, and even Byron, who are central to the novel's action. The final effect of two full chapters devoted to such dramatically irrelevant characters as the elder Hightowers and Burdens is more than just a heightening of confusion. For we come to see that not only do all the varied characters in the present situation bear a resemblance, but so do all the characters of the past; that Faulkner's view is not limited to a particular time and place; that it is not just the world of his contemporary South that is a puppet stage. The endless repetition and the eternal confusion of identity suggest that Faulkner is describing the human condition. The continuing geometrical pattern suggests that the mechanical force which turns characters into caricatures is eternal and absolute.

The pattern is complete when it includes Christmas. Christmas ironically concludes the list of proselytizers who invade the churches of the back hills. His relation to Hightower mirrors that of Nathaniel and Calvin Burden. His father, like Calvin's mother, is dark skinned. And just as Millie Hines furtively climbs through a window to elope with her lover, and Hightower's wife jumps through a window to escape both Hightower and the hotels of Memphis, and Lena climbs out her window to meet Brown, Christmas furtively climbs through windows to meet Bobbie Allen and Joanna. Christmas epitomizes all the confusion of race, religion, and sex. Like

Calvin Burden and the elder Hightower he kills a person over the Negro question. And like Joanna and Hightower his whole life is determined by a senseless killing that took place before he was born—the difference being that it was his father who was killed. Without a father, without a past, Christmas is not a caricature shaped by the senseless, rigid pattern of his history, but a puppet who is used to serve the senseless purposes of such caricatures. The dietician and Brown use the enigma of his race to save themselves; Hines and McEachern turn him into the object of their religious fanaticism; Joanna Burden uses his imagined darkness to serve the purpose of her religious and sexual rebellion.

But it is only when his comic potential is realized that Christmas fully becomes a puppet, and one way Faulkner accomplishes this is through the creation of a double in Brown. Faulkner's use of the double is more purely comic than Dostoyevsky's. Both of Faulkner's characters lack identity for opposite reasons—Christmas because he tries so hard to establish one, Brown because his life consists in evading one. Ironically Brown is white and Christmas, whose name suggests whiteness, is considered Negro; the irony is compounded when Brown is pictured with the darker skin. The unlikely partnership between two such contrary characters in their living quarters and bootlegging enterprise suggests an identity that is developed seriously when Brown becomes Christmas's pursuer, who is finally replaced by Percy Grimm. And it is developed comically when Mrs. Hines, Christmas's grandmother, mistakes Lena's baby—or Brown's mistake —for Christmas's. The comedy is complete when Lena herself almost comes to believe it.

The farce of Christmas's life is epitomized in chapter 5, where his entire history is recapitulated in a ritual that leads to the murder of Joanna Burden and to his own ironic definition. What initially precipitates this act is itself a comic mistake—Joanna thinks she is pregnant when she is really beginning menopause. The comic mistake can be seen as a cosmic joke—a central joke of the novel—in that death is taken for life. But the joke cannot arouse laughter, for when applied to Christmas it means that identity and destruction are one. In fact the joke inspires terror instead of laughter. Perhaps this is because, as Bergson suggests, comedy is traditionally based on a perversion of reality; we laugh when we see the world as it should not be. Faulkner, on the other hand, makes reality itself the source of his comedy; he shows us the joke of the world as it is. Even though we do not laugh, Christmas's action is ridiculous and the entire ritual is a parody.

The form of the ritual follows the shape of his life. It vacillates between violent extremes. The ritual begins at night, with negation, or rebellion against the alien limitations that have denied him a personality. First he rebels against Woman—the dietician, Mrs. McEachern, Bobbie Allen, Joanna, who fed him, lied for him, and because they were inconsistent, confused him. His rebellion takes the form of viciously, mechanically cutting off the new buttons of his underwear with the hard edge of his hand. Then he rebels against the White, who by turning him into a Negro has denied him his humanity: he walks naked into the headlights of an oncoming car, allowing his body to grow white out of the darkness, and shouts, "White bastards!" Later he rebels against the Negro, who has refused to accept him because of the color of his skin, and tries to walk down a whole jeering group of them. He also rebels against Sex—which has been confused with guilt and identified with violence—by choosing to sleep in the stable because horses are not women: "Even a mare horse is a kind of man." While in the context of the novel this sequence is not funny, its form is farcical, especially as we become aware that ex-

cept for a few derisive epithets it is all acted in pantomime. It takes on the quality of the kind of silent movie
which, though serious and gripping, contains a slapstick
dimension.

The rigid extremes of Christmas's life are further
dramatized when the rebellious night scenes are followed
by the mock-pastoral scene the next morning. The birds
are in "full chorus" and Christmas walks through the
dew-wet grass to a small valley with a running stream.
After a ritualistic washing and eating, Christmas sees the
"yellow day opening peacefully on before him, like a
corridor, an arras, into a still chiaroscuro without ur-
gency." The images, of course, carry exactly the opposite
implications of those Christmas has been living with and
will continue to live with all his life. Incongruously, they
call to mind Lena's journey in the beginning of the novel
along a "peaceful corridor paved with unflagging and
tranquil faith and peopled with kind and nameless faces
and voices." The quiet valley in which Christmas attains
his one moment of peace is unreal—as unreal as Lena's
journey—but it is unreal ironically because it is the only
organic setting in a world where reality is mechanical.
And the entire pastoral quality is mocked by the comic
picture of Christmas reading stories of sex and violence
with mechanical determination "to the last and final
page, to the last and final word."

After Christmas leaves the valley, light turns to darkness, and Faulkner's prose turns staccato and is punc-
tuated with time references: "At seven o'clock that evening he was in town, in a restaurant. . . . At nine o'clock
he was standing outside the barbershop." Time is another
mechanical and alien order imposed upon Christmas.
We are made aware of the difference between Lena's
world and the world of Jefferson by the increasing references to time as she approaches the city and by her
meeting with Byron Bunch—the timekeeper of the saw-

mill—who is her only link with the town and with Christmas. That time is unnatural and alien is further emphasized when we see McEachern, identified with a heavy silver timepiece, depriving young Christmas of an opportunity to wind his own watch, which he had to acquire surreptitiously. The mechanical movement of the watch accentuates the novel's naturalistic strain, the inevitable effect of past events, the reduction of all experience to rational quantity. Yet, as another mechanical force, it contributes to the novel's comic grid.

Christmas walks through the Negro section of town and then through the white section, which are neatly patterned and mutually exclusive, and which show him off as a mechanical doll with a "steady white shirt and pacing dark legs." The prose tempo increases, although Christmas moves with the same regularity. It is ten o'clock, eleven o'clock, twelve o'clock—and he moves toward Joanna's house not thinking but knowing, "*Something is going to happen. Something is going to happen to me.*"

The action of this chapter is central to the novel. The tone is grim and tense, and yet the picture we see is of a puppet being moved through a pantomime on a highly artificial stage. The incongruity between the tone and content, a kind of tall-tale technique in reverse, makes a mockery of ritual, rebellion, initiation, heroism, and life itself. And while it reflects the comic incongruity between the vital and the mechanical, it also shows us that this incongruity is the terrifying essence of reality.

The ritual is followed by a flashback to the scene where Christmas is caught getting sick on a tube of toothpaste while the dietician and intern make love. The juxtaposition of these two chapters yokes the two most important moments of Christmas's life—the first conscious moment of his existence, and the moment before he acts to define his essence. The radical time-shift dramatizes the difference between Christmas's subjective time pattern—the ordering of his unique vital force—and the pattern of clocktime, which disregards the individual and mechanizes the vital. In the scene at the orphanage, Christmas is wound up, as it were, and set in motion by the senseless fear of the dietician. This scene, too, is one of initiation, and the imposition of the arbitrary and rigid views of the adult upon the innocent child results in a confusion that shapes his psyche and determines that he will be a misfit. Sex is identified with food and nausea, security and guilt, money and punishment. Christmas is identified as a Negro for a reason unknown to him except that it is connected with sex. And when the "promissory note which he had signed with a tube of toothpaste" is recalled by McEachern, sex and race are identified with religious sin, all of which is given a threatening and legalistic cast, and Christmas is set off on the long street of his life over which he can have no control. Along this street he vacillates between the violent extremes that can have no connection in his consciousness; every choice he makes is a negation of the previous one. Given the life into which he has been forced, identity can only be negation. Therefore his one incontrovertible act is a choice of a double negation, darkness and death, and he commits himself to being a "nigger-murderer."

As his long street comes to an end, Christmas has the incongruous compulsion to eat fruit and corn and to calculate the day of the week and the time of the day. His rejection of food throughout the novel has been shown to be a rejection of Woman; his final compulsion to eat when he is most desperate to escape is a compulsion for life and shows that his past has been a series of life-denying gestures. His desperate need to find the order of time as he races from social authority emphasizes that life demands order. However the only order available to him is the absurd and life-denying order that has forced him to run in the first place. The cosmic joke of Faulkner's universe, like that of Kafka's, is that a rejection of its order leads to death, and an acceptance of it is a denial of humanity.

The punch line of the cosmic joke is Percy **Grimm**. His introduction at the end of the novel is indeed a bold stroke. Grimm is totally unconnected with any of the complex events in the novel; the accident of his being in Jefferson and the gratuitousness of his act give final emphasis to the wanton nature of Faulkner's world. Further, the particular situation is generalized since Grimm is of a different generation from the central characters and since he is not really pictured as a Southerner but more starkly as a Fascist whose religion of totalitarianism, racism, and nationalism resembles that of Mussolini and Hitler with frightening accuracy.

Yet we are not unprepared for Percy Grimm; he appears as a logical inevitability. His history reverberates with echoes from the lives of other characters. Like all the characters who have dominated Christmas's life, Grimm is a fanatic. But his extremism goes beyond that of the others, and when it transcends religion and white supremacy to insist that "the American is superior to all other white races and that the American uniform is superior to all men" it reaches the last ridiculous logical step. Further, Grimm's whole life, like that of Hightower and of Joanna, is dominated by the absurd accident of his being born too late, in his case for the First World War. But while all three characters missed out on an act of violence, the violence merely local for the others has become worldwide for Grimm—suggesting that he represents the logical extreme of negation.

Grimm is a caricature of all the caricatures in the novel. If he is the least funny it is because he is the least human. He is the most unsympathetically drawn character in all of Faulkner, and the most terrifying. In a universe that is wanton, Percy Grimm is the apostle of negation—a ridiculous figure with the power of an invulnerable machine. When we are told that his life has been as "uncomplex and inescapable as a barren corridor" we know that he is the logical character to destroy Christmas. And when Hightower, in his moment of recognition, perceives that Christmas and Grimm are two parts of the same person, the end of the joke is revealed.

The world of *Light in August* is finally pictured as a chessboard. As Brown tries to escape Lena without relinquishing his reward money, the characters with whom he has been involved and the money itself seem to him "just shapes like chessmen . . . unpredictable and without reason moved here and there by an Opponent who could read his moves before he made them and who created spontaneous rules which he and not the Opponent, must follow." These thoughts are out of character for Brown; but when we learn that Brown's escape succeeds at the very same time that Christmas's fails, we see the completed pattern of the double, through which Faulkner has been able to explore the varieties of human negation. Brown successfully escapes identity just as Christmas is killed trying to affirm one; the final image of Christmas collapsing into nothingness is the tragic counterpart to the comic image of Brown's escape, and it is not ameliorated by the spurious symbolism and rhetoric that follow.

This symmetry brings us back to the comic structure of the novel. The comic stage is finally reduced to a chessboard. The final simplification of the novel's intricate pattern may be likened to the resolution of a traditional comedy; but the chessboard is the ultimate structure for dehumanization. Brown succeeds after overcoming Byron's foolish attempt to live up to his namesake and be a hero. Christmas fails after Hightower's foolish attempt to be a martyr. Byron and Hightower do succeed in overcoming their past blindness and evasion. They do unselfishly choose to involve themselves in the lives of other people. They do go through the gestures of a hero and a martyr. In short they do everything possible to become human and to alter the course of events—but they are turned into fools by the world they inhabit. Like Brown's, Christmas's escape is described in terms of a chess game. That the "Player" is not pursuing Christmas but moving the pursuer and Christmas as well points up the terrifyingly absurd nature of Faulkner's world.

The simple pattern of the chessboard also emphasizes the naturalistic dimension of the novel, and indeed by the time Christmas is killed we are fully aware that every move in the game has been inevitable. The comic and the naturalistic are brought together in the image of the "Player." The final joke is that there is only one person playing the game, and that both Brown and Christmas, in fact all the characters, think they are players when they are really pawns.

What is most terrifying about this grotesque world is that all the fanatics turn out to be right, to be on the side of the absolute. Hines follows Millie and the circus man, McEachern chases Christmas and Bobbie Allen, Grimm pursues Christmas, with the same uncanny certainty. While all the fanatics in the novel deny human love in the name of a rigid principle, Grimm and Hines embody two dimensions of the absolute. Grimm, as we have seen, is the embodiment of total negation. Hines is the embodiment of total madness. The most incredible character in the novel—preaching white supremacy to Negroes week after week, keeping the doctor from his daughter as she dies in childbirth, presiding over Christmas's young life like some kind of dark force—he becomes fully believable. Everything that the mad Hines prophesies comes true. He is all-knowing and all-power-ful.

While Faulkner shows most of the characters in *Light in August* to be rigid or fanatic, he never shows them to be as inhuman as Grimm or as mad as Hines. They represent the bulk of humanity, for whom Faulkner has varying degrees of sympathy. They are not hypocrites but individuals furiously trying to achieve some kind of stability and order. They are grotesques, but not like Sherwood Anderson's who take to themselves a small part of the total truth; for in Faulkner's world there is no total truth. It is part of the joke of Faulkner's universe that these people turn grotesque not by denying their humanity but by asserting it. And the joke is compounded, for by seizing onto a small part of the total senseless pattern, they contribute to the dynamic of the mad machine in control. In the universe of *Light in August* the governing force combines the powers of those forces discussed in chapters 1 and 2—it is both transcendent and immanent. The legalism, the rigid and exclusive categories, the very symbolism of black and white that dramatizes the duality of sex, religion, and race, are all created by members of society for psychological survival. And the result, as Jan Kott describes the world of the grotesque, is similar to the way the scrambling people contribute to the momentum of the funhouse "barrel of laughs."

Lena Grove is immune to the forces of Faulkner's world and serves as a polar contrast to the other characters, but it is wrong to see her as a pastoral ideal. For despite her associations with nature, religion, wholeness, and innocence, she is the most ridiculous character in the novel. She is completely irrelevant to the real world of Jefferson, which Faulkner so vividly describes, and shows no awareness of the violence and tragedy that surround her. She even parodies the main themes of the novel. Her lovemaking is as furtive as Christmas's; she, too, is identified with the road; and she seeks her lover along it with the uncanny certainty of a Hines, a McEachern, or a Percy Grimm. The wheels with which she is associated parody the shape of Christmas's long street that ends in a circle and the wheel of Hightower's vision; the child to whom she gives birth is a parody of Christmas; and her association with birth and fertility is an ironic travesty of the destructive violence and sterility of the whole novel. Even as an ideal she is a parody, for she is shown to be more animal than human, and she endures only because she is totally devoid of human sensibility.

Two characters gain a kind of dignity in the world of *Light in August*, but only at the expense of appearing foolish. Hightower began by substituting a mad dream for a mad reality, and this enabled him to evade commitment. When he does assert his humanity, his relation to others is shown to be even more ridiculous than his mad dream. When he lies for Christmas he repudiates the rigid system that has enabled him to survive; but however heroic, his act is too late, irrelevant, and absurd. When he finally comes to recognize the truth about his life, that not only was he the instrument of his wife's death but that he was a "figure antic as a showman," and when he comes to understand the relationship of all the events and all the characters, he is close to madness or death. The wheel of his vision is symbolic of life's organic nature but also of the annihilation of the rigid rationality necessary for human living.

Byron Bunch becomes an almost totally comic fool. He shares the novel's final scene with Lena, but in contrast to Lena he does develop a sensibility. He began by evading reality, spending each Saturday at the sawmill and each Sunday leading a choir in the back hills to keep out of trouble. Like all the other characters in Jefferson, he simplified his life by resorting to a moral legalism.

But his legalism was shown to be ridiculously ineffective as he became the main link between all the characters in the novel. Byron finally chooses to accept reality and to become fully involved in the lives of other people. In the scene of Brown's escape and especially in the concluding scenes with Lena, he is portrayed as a fool in the tradition of the buffoon. Enid Welsford, in her study of *The Fool: His Social and Literary History*, describes the buffoon, who appeared in stories told among simple people and who preceded the court fool and the literary fool. One of the two types of buffoons was a peasant or small tradesman. He was physically undignified, incapable of foresight or prudence, single-minded, and, being more simple than those to whom his stories were told, gave the listeners a sense of superiority. But he also inspired them with his resiliency, freedom, and, most important, his ability to break down "the distinction . . . between folly and wisdom." By portraying Byron as a buffoon foolishly trying to assume responsibility and achieve human connection in a world that denies these possibilities, Faulkner realizes the redemptive potential of comedy and foolishness.

The opening and closing chapters frame the novel by their incongruity with its center. They are incongruous because the setting is outside of Jefferson and because the focus is on Lena, who is totally unaffected by the main action that takes place there. But the greatest incongruity is in the tone and perspective. Part of the first chapter and all of the last are told from the viewpoints of detached observers who can see the humor. Hence these chapters are the most purely comic, and the final chapter draws together the novel's entire comic pattern. Armstid, with his folklore knowledge of the eternal woman, foreshadows the furniture dealer, who tells the story of Byron's and Lena's courtship to his wife —as a joke. He parodies the fanatics of Mottstown and

Jefferson in his comic single-mindedness and in using the story as a means to his own salacious end. In so doing he brings the novel to a close with a double parody of the marriage procession of traditional comedy—a parody as cruel as Dostoyevsky's when he pictures Myshkin and Rogozhin lying together alongside the dead Nastasya, and Kafka's when he unites the Samsa family after the death of their disgusting bug, and when he shows Joseph K. reaching out his arms toward the first sign of human help at the moment he is killed like a dog.

Byron decides that he has come too far to quit trying for Lena, and the final image is of Lena feeding the baby in the back of the truck, "watching the telephone poles and the fences passing like it was a circus parade." This image reiterates the novel's major motifs for the last time: Lena is the symbol of sex, the feeding mother, and Christianity; the telephone poles and fence posts have lined the street along which Christmas has been kept running; and the speeding truck suggests the pun on "race" that has brought about his destruction. The final reference to the circus emphasizes how Faulkner's world makes all human effort ridiculous—and that Byron Bunch, its most attractive and admirable character, will never be more than a buffoon, or fool.

Faulkner's view of the world is terrifying but it is not pessimistic. Quite the contrary. The greatness of Faulkner's novel is that it not only accepts the world but affirms it. And while the affirmation is not that of traditional comedy, since he subverts its devices, it is the affirmation of the *commedia dell'arte* and the pantomime stage. Byron Bunch does develop; he develops from a puppet to a fool, from a ridiculous caricature to a character who is laughable. And if a puppet is distinguished by his mechanical rigidity, a fool is marked by his flexibility and resiliency. Enid Welsford concludes that clowns and fools not only resist physical laws in their acrobatics and in their ability to appear none the worse after a beating, but they resist the laws of social convention, evoking in the audience "a sudden sense of pressure relieved, of a birth of new joy and freedom." And she expresses the only conclusion we can draw from Faulkner's novel, that "this kind of emancipation . . . can be won only by the saint in ecstasy, or by the fool in jest, never by the revolutionary in earnest."

5

The World Upside Down I
Flannery O'Connor

When we begin to read a story or a novel by Flannery O'Connor we find the characters flat, the satire obvious, the violence all out of proportion; yet almost every work remains hauntingly memorable. The full impact is delayed; it is not until sometime after we finish that the multiple dimensions explode into view. One reason for this is, as Melvin Friedman puts it, "She forces us to go through a complete Cartesian purgation; our minds are cleansed of all previous notions. When we have forgotten the other books we have read, we can then allow for the existence of Hazel Motes (*Wise Blood*), Rayber (*The Violent Bear It Away*), The Misfit ('A Good Man Is Hard To Find') and Mary Grace ('Revelation')." The other reason can be discovered by examining one of her most simple stories, "The Comforts of Home," which appears in her posthumous collection.

In this story we are introduced to three cardboard characters: Thomas, the cynical intellectual tied to his mother's home by the cord of his electric blanket; his mother, a middle-class woman who believes in all the clichés; and Sarah Ham, alias Star Drake, a cheap, rootless "nimpermaniac," whose picture in the paper has drawn Thomas's mother to the county jail with a box of candy, and who finally comes to live with them. Clear-eyed Thomas is right and his sentimental mother is wrong; Star is a slut and an opportunist, and she is contemptuous of the mother's charitable advances. But

although Thomas's judgments are rationally correct, his
lack of charity is shown to be abhorrent and to drive Star
to more destruction. As Star becomes an irrational threat
to both the sentimental and rational orders of the house-
hold, we find our attitudes shifting from judgment to
sympathy. We come to understand how Star is drawn to
destruction by her need for love, how the mother's honest compassion cannot suffice because it is channeled
into meaningless clichés, how Thomas's rejection of Star
(by now the ironic symbolism of the name is clear) is a
result of his attachment to his mother, which is itself a
result of the clichés that have formed his mother's world.
The situation develops into a triangle like that in Sartre's
No Exit, except that Miss O'Connor shows us what
happens when one character leaves.

When Thomas discovers the pistol missing from his
desk drawer, he is urged by the voice of his dead father,
the original owner of the pistol and the man Thomas
could never be, to go to the sheriff. Thomas acts, but on
returning home he finds the gun back in its place. Out-
raged, desperate, driven by the voice of his father, he
tries to plant the gun in Star's purse—but Star catches
him in the act. The mother refuses to believe that her
son, a gentleman, would do anything like that. She
throws herself between Thomas and Star to protect her
son from being strangled. At the same moment, acting
on his father's command, Thomas fires; and the blast
that is meant to end the evil in the world and "shatter
the laughter of sluts" kills his mother. But suddenly the
perspective is changed. We view the scene through the
eyes of the sheriff, who has just entered the door. His
brain works "like a calculating machine." He sees the
facts as clearly as if they were already in the newspaper:
boy kills mother, having planned to pin it on the girl.
And further scrutiny reveals further insight: "Over her
body, the killer and the slut were about to collapse into

each other's arms." The sheriff knows a "nasty bit" when he sees it.

Flannery O'Connor's strategy is just this: as the threat of violence and the irrational increases, our cold judgment turns to human understanding, caricatures turn into characters. The moment of our deepest understanding coincides with the moment of the most irrational destruction—and the characters are turned back into caricatures, human beings are frozen into comic-strip outline by an objective and irrelevant observer. The observer in this story is the sheriff who comes in from the outside; more often it is the narrator. Because of the double point of view, the culminating destruction contains elements of senseless terror and slapstick comedy. The effect is explosive, an apocalyptic turning of the world upside down. Not only are all the clichés destroyed but our very foundations for rational and moral judgment are annihilated. And—most unexpectedly—in the harshest light we realize the fullest sympathy.

Think of the two contradictory impressions we have of the grandmother in "A Good Man Is Hard To Find," the one of our initial reading and the one gained by reflecting from the vantage of the story's ending. Shocked into a moment of intense compassion we remember the grandmother with both contempt and sympathy. We judge her as egocentric and stupid for directing Bailey down the wrong road in the wrong state, just to satisfy a whim; but on reflection we sympathize with an old woman's desire to relive a childhood memory. We judge her responsible for the car's overturning, but we remember the comic pathos of the lonely widow's stowaway cat leaping onto Bailey's shoulder. We judge her responsible for waving down the strangers in their "big black battered hearse-like automobile," but we are horrified when she brings forth the Misfit.

The technique which Flannery O'Connor uses from

the story's structure, to the individual scene, down to the descriptive paragraph depends upon the comic surprise at the end which startles us into a contradictory attitude. The initial description of the Misfit, emerging slowly like a photograph in a developing tray, turns disproportion into incongruity, caricature into a conjunction of misrelated parts, curiosity into terror.

The driver got out of the car and stood by the side of it, looking down at them. He was an older man than the other two. His hair was just beginning to gray and he wore silver-rimmed spectacles that gave him a scholarly look. He had a long creased face and didn't have on any shirt or undershirt. He had on blue jeans that were too tight for him and was holding a black hat and a gun. The two boys also had guns.

It is not until the last word of the penultimate sentence that we see the gun; we are surprised by its appearing so late in the description and so matter-of-factly as the last of three items of dress (the second one we now see as the stereotype-villain's black hat). Then, to fix the impression in our minds with the same quality of irrelevant detail, Miss O'Connor casually brings out that "the two boys also had guns." The description is calculated to startle us into experiencing the terror of the commonplace, but it also follows the pattern of the grandmother's and of the reader's developing awareness. The awareness develops slowly, first, because it is so absolutely beyond normal expectation, and, second, because of the psychic struggle to refuse it. The grandmother and the reader fight against accepting raw reality; the grandmother alone, unloved, and vulnerable has developed a language of clichés to disguise and control reality much the same way that the reader has developed a set of literary responses.

In the final scene Hiram and Bobby Lee have just taken June Star and her mother into the woods to be shot, and the grandmother is alone with the Misfit, who is now wearing Bailey's yellow shirt with the bright blue parrots and discoursing in a gentlemanly way about Jesus being like him except for His not committing any crime. Miss O'Connor has developed her story to the point beyond which the "suspension of disbelief" would be impossible, the characters having the barest resemblance to human beings. And at this moment we can see the grandmother most clearly and understand her with the most feeling. When she tells the Misfit that she knows he's a good man, that he has good blood in him, that he ought to pray, she is using the only words she knows to deal with the situation, to express her fears, to exorcize the threat. The comic incongruity of her phrases emphasizes her impotence and the irrationality of the threat. When she concludes with the recognition, "Why you're one of my babies. You're one of my own children!" she is expressing, although not admitting to herself, an acceptance of the irrational and an admission of a connection with it, and consequently of her culpability. When we watch the Misfit respond to her touch by shooting her three times in the chest, and then putting his gun down to wipe his glasses clean, and when we hear him tell Bobby Lee that "she would of been a good woman . . . if it had been somebody there to shoot her every minute of her life"—we forgive her everything.

All Flannery O'Connor's stories depend upon a final jarring but comic incongruity. It is just when her characters are most grotesque that we see them as most human, when they are frozen into lifeless attitudes that they appear most lifelike. There is just a moment, brief but intense, and this moment effects a violent disturbance in the reader, a radical change of response that will turn the recollection into a new story. In "The River" a child drowns himself seeking the Kingdom of Heaven; the last thing he sees is the head of Mr. Paradise, appearing from time to time on the surface of the water. But Bevel is ultimately baptized and is reborn in our imaginations due to his poignant understanding of this mystery. Hulga, the pedantic Ph.D., is seduced and left stranded in the loft by a wily Bible salesman who only wants to make off with her false leg. In the end satire is subordinated to the agony of loneliness. In "The Artificial Nigger" we come to understand the depths of betrayal, forgiveness, and communion, when, after their journey and trial in the big city, Mr. Head and his grandson are reunited in astonishment and awe at the sight of a plaster Negro. "Mr. Head opened his lips to make a lofty statement and heard himself say, 'They ain't got enough real ones here. They got to have an artificial one.'" In "Greenleaf" the complacent Mrs. May tries to coerce her shiftless employee into shooting his sons' stray bull that has been destroying her property, and she is accidentally gored to death embracing the destructive horns. In "A View of the Woods" Mr. Fortune tries to "save" his granddaughter from her cruel and stupid father, and ends by smashing her head in a fight that resembles a love bout. In "The Lame Shall Enter First" Sheppard discovers his son, whom he neglected in order to save a demoniac delinquent, hanging from an attic beam, after the boy had tried to fly to his dead mother. In "Revelation" smug and proper Mrs. Turpin comes to see herself as a wart hog. In "Parker's Back" O. E. Parker, with a fresh, sore Byzantine Christ tattooed on his back, is shown crying beneath a pecan tree. In "Judgment Day" Tanner, who had been proud of his ability to boss Negroes in Georgia, is forced to retire to his daughter's New York apartment; alone and unwanted he is drawn to the only symbol of home, a Negro actor who lives next door. But the Negro, taking Tanner's approaches as an insult, beats him, and Tanner is found dead, with his hat pulled down over his face and his head and arms thrust through the spokes of a bannister.

In each case we are prepared for the apocalyptic image by a portent of irrational threat presented with comic detachment. The threat has little effect on the characters, for they have developed blinders to the possibilities of human life. The world is turned upside down by a comic surprise, and in each case, with the apocalypse, human value is unexpectedly asserted in a world without meaning.

Most critics judge Flannery O'Connor to be essentially a writer of short stories, but it is in her novels that we see her world in all its breadth and complexity. Enoch Emery of *Wise Blood*, one of Miss O'Connor's most successful minor creations, alone in the city, baffled by its novelties, furious at its impersonality and its impenetrable mysteries, is a grotesque parody of the already grotesque hero, Hazel Motes. Both characters are intensely in search of what they consider the new Jesus. Just before Enoch is inspired to ascend personally in the form of Gonga, the Giant Jungle Monarch, he recalls something that happened to him when he was four years old. "His father had brought him home a tin box from the penitentiary. It was orange and had a picture of some peanut brittle on the outside of it and green letters that said, A NUTTY SURPRISE! When Enoch had opened it, a coiled piece of steel had sprung out at him and broken off the ends of his two front teeth. His life was full of so many happenings like that that it would seem he should have been more sensitive to his times of danger." That life is full of "nutty surprises" coming from sources of love and authority is the cause of Enoch's comic rage at everything and everyone. His absurd and extravagant gestures—stealing the shrunken mummy, becoming a gorilla—are attempts to get at the mysterious source of these surprises, to comprehend it, to get beyond its threat, to become one with it.

That life is full of nutty surprises is also the source of Sabbath Hawkes's confusion. In search for some guide besides her phony blind preacher father, she writes to "this woman in the [newspaper] that tells you what to do when you don't know. . . . 'Dear Mary, I am a bastard and a bastard shall not enter the kingdom of heaven as we all know, but I have this personality that makes boys follow me. Do you think I should neck or not? I shall not enter the kingdom of heaven anyway so I don't see what difference it makes.'" While Enoch Emery is drawn to the gorilla because it was the first being that extended its hand to him since he has been in the city, Sabbath Hawkes is drawn to Hazel because of the surprise that has made him available.

That life is full of nutty surprises is also the source of Hazel's conflict of wills. In her 1962 introduction to the novel, Flannery O'Connor tells us that Hazel's freedom, and freedom in general, "does not mean one will, but many wills conflicting in one man." Pirandello also emphasizes man's multiplicity in his "Art of Humor." "We have within us four or five souls in conflict with one another," and while the epic or dramatic writer "composes" a character by harmonizing the elements, the humorist "breaks down" the character into his contradictory elements; "whereas the former takes pains to have him consistent in every act, the latter enjoys representing him in his incongruities." What Pirandello does not acknowledge in his essay but does express in his dramatic works is the contradictoriness of the world beyond the self. What Flannery O'Connor does not acknowledge in her introduction but dramatizes fully in her novel is the relationship between Hazel's conflicting wills and the nutty surprises in his life. He remembers his grandfather as "a circuit preacher, a waspish old man who had ridden over three counties with Jesus hidden in his head like a stinger," and who "when it was time to bury him, they shut the top of his box down and he didn't make a move." And he remembers his two brothers, one who

died as an infant, and the other who was killed at age
seven by a mowing machine. When he was eighteen the
army took him away from Eastrod, Tennessee; "he saw
the war as a trick to lead him into temptation." But,
"the army sent him halfway around the world and forgot
him. He was wounded and they remembered him long
enough to take the shrapnel out of his chest—they said
they took it out but they never showed it to him and he
felt it still in there, rusted, and poisoning him—and then
they sent him to another desert and forgot him again."
When he was released he returned to find his home
deserted, decayed into a shell, and looted completely
except for a chifforobe and two lengths of wrapping cord.
His response to this nutty surprise, which leaves him
abandoned in a world of mystery and threat, is the comic
aggression that will continue to characterize him
throughout the novel. He ties the cabinet to the floor-
boards with the wrapping cord and leaves a note in each
drawer: "THIS SHIFFER-ROBE BELONGS TO
HAZEL MOTES. DO NOT STEAL IT OR YOU
WILL BE HUNTED DOWN AND KILLED." The
comic aggression results from the inner contradictions of
his wanting to conserve what he feels to be worthless.
His immediate departure for the city suggests that he
wants equally as much to seek out the threat to his old
values, not to destroy it but to join forces with it.

His ambivalence toward the world which holds attractive and threatening mysteries is epitomized in the scene
of his entrance into the city and a new life. Wearing a
stiff black preacher's hat and a glaring blue suit with the
price tag still stapled on the sleeve, Haze leaves the train
and enters a room marked "MEN'S TOILET.
WHITE" where he finds the name of Mrs. Leora Watts
written on the wall. When he arrives at her house, he
peeks through a crack in the door to see a "big woman
with very yellow hair and white skin that glistened with

a greasy preparation," wearing a small-sized pink nightgown and cutting her toenails with a large pair of scissors. She looks up at him and then returns to her toenails. He enters the disordered room, walks over to the bureau, and fingers the nail file and empty jelly glasses, then steps over to her bed, sits down on the edge, picks up her heavy foot and moves it to one side. "Mrs. Watts's mouth split in a wide full grin that showed her teeth. They were small and pointed and speckled with green and there was a wide space between each one. She reached out and gripped Haze's arm just above the elbow. 'You huntin' something?' she drawled."

To Haze the world is "fantastic" (in Sartre's sense of the word), but Flannery O'Connor, in contrast to Dickens and Kafka, shows us that this view is restricted to her protagonist. The humor, which pervades this scene and the rest of the novel until Haze blinds himself, derives from the incongruity of the boy's single-minded action in a setting that will clearly not provide the goal he is seeking. Mrs. Watts's room is a microcosm of the world of *Wise Blood*, which is filled with objects and people that offer promises to Haze of mystery and meaning. The promises are attractive to Haze because they come from a source beyond the only life that he has known, but for the same reason they signal danger. The inarticulation of Haze's view and reality creates a world full of nutty surprises. The attraction and repulsion of this world lead to a behavior that is at once belligerent and guarded; it is comic because of this ambivalence, and because we are aware that nothing in the scene can provide the danger Haze anticipates. But we are also aware that nothing in the scene—in the world of *Wise Blood*—can offer the kind of promise Haze is so desperately seeking.

The irrational violence that later ensues seems to be the direct consequence of Haze's incongruous behavior.

A patrolman gratuitously pushes Haze's car over the embankment. But this is after Haze rams the false Prophet's car into the ditch and runs him over, mechanically, back and forth. In the end two policemen find Haze blind and sick in a drainage ditch, and one of them, "perceiving that he was conscious, hit him over the head with his new billy. 'We don't want to have no trouble with him,' he said." But this was after Haze blinded himself with lye, tied barbed wire around his chest, and walked around with broken glass in his shoes.

We are now at the low point of the novel. The world has become exhausted of all mystery and of all hope. Hazel Motes has turned his violence inward and irrationally takes upon himself the guilt for the sins of the world. But at this low point the upside-down world is once more comically inverted—and Hazel Motes himself becomes the last nutty surprise. The landlady, who has begun by exploiting her blind tenant for his disability check, and who then plans to marry him and have him committed to the state insane asylum, gradually decides to keep him with her, and ends with an outrageously absurd monologue, another parody of the marriage ritual that is nonetheless one of the most poignant expressions of love in modern literature.

He died in the squad car but they didn't notice and took him on to the landlady's. She had them put him on her bed and when she had pushed them out the door, she locked it behind them and drew up a straight chair and sat down close to his face where she could talk to him. "Well, Mr. Motes," she said, "I see you've come home!"

His face was stern and tranquil. "I knew you'd come back," she said. "And I've been waiting for you. And you needn't to pay any more rent but have it free here, any way you like, upstairs or down. Just however you want it and with me to wait on you, or if you want to go on somewhere, we'll both go."

She had never observed his face more composed and she grabbed his hand and held it to her heart. It was resistless and dry. The outline of a skull was plain under his skin and the deep burned eye sockets seemed to lead into the dark tunnel where he had disappeared. She leaned closer and closer to his face, looking deep into them, trying to see how she had been cheated or what had cheated her, but she couldn't see anything. She shut her eyes and saw the pin point of light but so far away that she could not hold it steady in her mind. She felt as if she were blocked at the entrance of something. She sat staring with her eyes shut, into his eyes, and felt as if she had finally got to the beginning of something she couldn't begin, and she saw him moving farther and farther away, farther and farther into the darkness until he was the pin point of light.

While the humor, the tragedy, and the final poignancy of *Wise Blood* result from the discrepancy between expectations and capricious reality, the same elements in *The Violent Bear It Away* result from the clashing of opposites. Haze lives in a world populated by Mrs. Watts, Enoch Emery, Asa Hawkes, Sabbath Hawkes, Hoover Shoats, a false replica of himself, a landlady, and a number of patrolmen. Whether the characters hold out promises to Haze or whether they use Haze for their own ends, they all exist more or less on an equal plane, creating a capricious environment, and contributing to the novel's loose structure, which many fastidious critics hold to be a major flaw. Francis Marion Tarwater, on the other hand, lives in a world clearly divided into the terrains of Old Tarwater and Rayber; the minor characters are well subordinated, the novel's tight structure reinforces the central division.

When, in an essay written for Granville Hicks's *The Living Novel*, Flannery O'Connor implicitly criticized the infectious "Manichaean spirit of the times," she did so as a Catholic for whom this kind of dualism is heresy, and as a woman of deep compassion who saw the errors and dangers in dividing the world between light and dark. In *The Violent Bear It Away* she used what, at the risk of a theological oversimplification, we could call the Manichaean conflict as a device to concentrate her view of the modern condition and to create another variation of turning the world upside down. With her comic instincts she could exploit the ludicrous and irrational elements of the Manichaean struggle. The comedy results in a deepening of psychological complexity and a heightening of apocalyptic terror.

Old Tarwater was the man of mystery and fanatic religion, Rayber is the man of reason. The fourteen-year-old boy tells his uncle Rayber how he defied the old man's command to be buried: "He was eating his breakfast and I never moved him from the table. I set him on fire where he was and the house with him. . . . He's reduced to ashes. He don't even have a cross set up over him. If it's anything left of him, the buzzards wouldn't have it and the bones the dogs'll carry off. That's how dead he is." And when Rayber commends him "the boy's pride swelled, 'I done the needful,' he said." But when the schoolteacher, with his hearing aid and his "drill-like eyes," continues with enthusiasm, "It's not too late for me to make a man of you. . . . You and I will make up for lost time," Tarwater's "expression hardened until it was a fortress wall to keep his thoughts from being exposed."

Tarwater is caught between the religious fanatic and the schoolteacher much the same way as Joe Christmas in Faulkner's *Light in August* is caught between the categories of black and white: he is compelled to choose one, he is drawn to both, neither is finally relevant to his inner needs. One difference between the two novels is that while Christmas is excluded from the alternative categories by the powers of his world, the powers of Tarwater's world struggle to win him. Nevertheless, the alternatives for Tarwater are as humanly impossible as Christmas's. Miss O'Connor shows them to be impossible through her comic treatments.

She caricatures Old Tarwater in slapstick scenes: the wild old man shooting at Rayber when he and the welfare woman come to rescue the boy; the stubborn character arguing with the lawyer over his father's will; the literalistic grandfather instructing young Tarwater how to roll his big dead body down the stairs and to the edge of the grave, and then to prop it up with bricks, lest it tumble in during the digging. All through his life Old Tarwater is pictured as an absurd fanatic, and in his death he becomes a cartoon figure: "At the moment of his death, he sat down to his breakfast and lifted his knife in one square red hand halfway to his mouth, and then with a look of complete astonishment, he lowered it until the hand rested on the edge of the plate and tilted it up off the table. . . . His mouth twisted down sharply on one side and he remained exactly as he was, perfectly balanced, his back a good six inches from the chair back and his stomach caught just under the edge of the table. His eyes, dead silver, were focussed on the boy across from him."

Rayber too is given the full comic treatment. We remember Tarwater's reaction when his "eyes followed the wires of the hearing aid down to the metal box stuck in his belt. 'What you wired for?' he drawled. 'Does your head light up?'" And later, "Do you think in the box . . . or do you think in your head?" And we remember the scene of Rayber with his pajama top stuck in his trousers, barefooted, and jaw set, following Tarwater along the streets and alleys to the revival meeting and spying through the window until Lucette Carmody, the child evangelist, points him out, "I see a dead man Jesus hasn't raised. His head is in the window but his ear is deaf to the Holy Word."

The comic treatments of Old Tarwater and Rayber are different: the old fanatic is rendered comic by vital exaggeration, the schoolteacher by mechanical diminution. However both comic treatments work to render each character as an impossible human alternative. This does not mean that they are any the less potent in their effects on young Tarwater. Quite the contrary; this is all there is for the boy—there is no other choice. Moreover, there is an underlying relationship between the two. It is the nature of Manichaean conflict that the choice of one side cannot be an abrogation of the other—until the conflict ends darkness cannot be without light, and the choice of light entails the continual awareness of dark. The wild mystic and the rationalist schoolteacher are defined in terms of each other. When Tarwater burns his great-uncle, he does it in the same spirit of religious fanaticism that Old Tarwater would have required in the burial. When he kills Bishop, he does it for the same religious reason that is necessary for the baptism. When he chooses to become a prophet, he must go to the evil city to save souls.

By treating the conflict of opposites comically, Flannery O'Connor emphasizes their irreconcilable opposition and the apparently incongruous fact of their interrelationship. Moreover, she takes her characters and the positions they hold beyond the realm of possible human choice. Young Tarwater is also given full comic treatment, but rather than being exaggerated like the old man or diminished like the schoolteacher, he is created as a Bergsonian caricature in reverse. Like those writers previously discussed, especially Faulkner, Flannery O'Connor achieves her humor by disclosing the human within the mechanical. In a world dominated by equal and opposite forces, human beings are turned into mechanical puppets. It is a triumph for humanity that the human element is not totally destroyed but can still assert itself. This kind of turning the world upside down is nothing short of what the Catholic might term a miracle. By his unreasonable stubbornness and integrity, Francis Marion Tarwater has done the impossible; the joke is not on St. Francis and Mary after all. He has done the impossible by choosing the most impossible of the alternatives—to follow Old Tarwater and become a prophet. As Miss O'Connor once stated, "Old Tarwater is the hero of *The Violent Bear It Away,* and I'm right behind him 100 percent."

Flannery O'Connor was not advocating Tarwater's fanaticism; this is obvious from her sustained comic treatment which enables us to see how ridiculous and how destructive this fanaticism can be. But turning the Tarwaters into saints is the only possibility in a world as negative as the one she describes. It is important to remember some of the characters outside the family who represent the rest of society: Meeks, who uses love to sell copper flues; the welfare woman, who deserts Rayber, leaving him with their idiot child; the truck driver who listens to Tarwater's confessions only to keep awake; and the homosexual who rapes Tarwater in the woods. What is needed in a world so totally negative and so irrationally in conflict is a total reversal, a transvaluation of values, and it is precisely this that Flannery O'Connor achieves in the end. She is even more successful than Graham Greene in communicating the nonrational nature of religious commitment. Rayber is right to deny the irrational force of love that surges up in him from time to time, and Tarwater is foolish to allow this force to gain control. But Tarwater is no more foolish than Erasmus' Christian Fool or Plato's foolish Socrates, in whose tradition Miss O'Connor followed more closely than any other modern writer—by creating her own foolish idiom.

By recalling this tradition briefly we may gain an important perspective by which to measure her achievement. When we read a Platonic Dialogue for the first time we feel, like Meno, the joy of discovering a truth that was all the while before us. Plato achieves this success by presenting a dramatic character who destroys the familiar world, deprives us of our prefabricated security, and returns us to an intellectual virginity where we can think again with clarity and precision. Erasmus accomplishes the same end by presenting Folly, who continually changes her guise, now being the inspiration of humane action, now the goad to arrogance, now the source of Christian commitment. In his *Praisers of Folly*, Walter Kaiser points out that by creating a fool as his protagonist, Plato affirms the classical view of the world as a stage and life as a play. A play is a kind of playing which, Kaiser continues, is defined by formality, pattern, and rules. The Dialectic is a formal game in which Socrates, the wise man playing the fool, ravages an accepted truth by exploring its antithesis—or he turns the world upside down; *The Praise of Folly* is a formal game where the irony is elaborately compounded. The result is a rediscovery of essential truth or a transvaluation of values.

In her stories and in each of her novels Flannery O'Connor uses the same comic strategy of turning the world upside down. In her stories it is to effect a fresh moment of insight and compassion, in *Wise Blood* it is to depict the search for meaning in a capricious world, in *The Violent Bear It Away* it is to depict the search for meaning in a world polarized by an irrational and irreconcilable dualism. In each case Flannery O'Connor turns the world upside down to shock us into a clear perception of a universe that is totally negative and violently irrational. And then through another surprise and inversion she rediscovers and redefines old values and demonstrates the possibility of compassion and meaning.

6

The World Upside Down II
William Burroughs's *Naked Lunch* and Nabokov's *Lolita*

The game of turning the world upside down can be played toward an end other than the one initiated by Plato and Erasmus, and continued in our time by Flannery O'Connor in all of her stories and novels. Ernst Curtius, in his *European Literature and the Latin Middle Ages*, classifies "The World Upside Down" as a conventional rhetorical topic, which is exemplified in a poem of the *Carmina Burana*. The poem begins with a complaint that youth no longer studies and learning is in decay. And soon the idea develops that the whole world is topsy-turvy: "The blind lead the blind and hurl themselves into the abyss; birds fly before they are fledged; the ass plays the lute; oxen dance; plough boys turn soldiers. The Fathers Gregory, Jerome, Augustine, and the Father of the Monks, Benedict, are to be found in the ale house, in court, or in the meat market. Mary no longer delights in the contemplative life nor Martha in the active. Leah is Barren, Rachel blear-eyed. Cato haunts the stews, Lucretia has turned whore. What was once outlawed is now praised. Everything is out of joint." This is clearly a different game from that played in the *Dialogues* and *The Praise of Folly*. It results in a mad dream world, where there is no transvaluation of values, no surprising affirmation of old order and value, but sheer destruction and chaos.

84

However, despite the destruction and chaos, there is a positive joy of released creative energy. This is the same joy that pervades the Roman Saturnalia and the Kalends of January. In the Christian Middle Ages it also takes the form of blasphemous license in the Feast of Fools. According to a contemporary description quoted by Curtius, "Priests and clerks may be seen wearing masks and monstrous visages at the hours of office. They dance in the choir dressed as women, panders or minstrels. They sing wanton songs. They eat black puddings at the horn of the altar while the celebrant is saying mass. They play at dice there. They cense with stinking smoke from the soles of old shoes. They run and leap through the church, without a blush at their own shame. Finally they drive about the town and its theaters in shabby traps and carts; and rouse the laughter of their fellows and the bystanders in infamous performances, with indecent gestures and verses scurrilous and unchaste."

The Feast of Fools was an English New Year's revel; in France the fool was expelled from the church, but year-round fool societies were formed which had license to satirize and generally mock the established order. The *Sociétés Joyeuses*, as they were called, formalized their mockery in fool, or *sotie*, dramas, which attacked the ills and abuses of society in attitudes ranging from bitter condemnation, to comic ridicule, to philosophic acceptance of folly as fact. Enid Welsford describes how in spirit the early *soties* were close to pure fantasy; folly was not a symbol for vice but a catalyst to free the imagination and to melt the solid structure of the world. And even though the *soties* become more bitter, the dramatic elements always function to destroy the spectator's sense of reality. Cap and bells suggest a complete irrelevance to everyday living. Dialogue shifts into incoherent banter or nonsense verse (there is a passage in the Rouen *Menus propos* that sounds like Ionesco's *Bald*

Soprano). The actors are skilled acrobats who, when they turn a handspring in the midst of their banter, defy the laws of gravity and grammar at once. All of this contributes to the impending chaos, which climaxes a turbulent battle of the fools. The world is turned upside down, and while the fools have brought about complete destruction, they have also provided the maximum opportunity for play—for a foolish activity without utilitarian, ethical, or teleological motivation, but, as I hope to show in the concluding chapter, a manifestation of the humane spirit.

The injection of farce into the medieval miracle plays is often rationalized as a comic relief for the spectator who had to stand for several days through a dramatization of the world's history. But the idea of relief hardly explains the slapstick scenes that are integral to the best plays. Cain in the Towneley *Abel* is wonderfully vital in his obscene reply to his brother's unctious greeting and in his dialogue with Garcio while burying Abel's body; in the York version he beats the angel who comes to ask after Abel. Noah's wife makes her husband seem ridiculous when, after all his strenuous labor, she tells him she can't tell the front from the rear of the ark, and that she won't come aboard till she completes her spinning. And Noah, a medieval model of dignity and pattern for Christ, becomes a henpecked husband who like a naughty child is scolded by his son before climbing to the helm and reassuming his role as patriarch. In the *Second Shepherds' Play*, the brief adoration scene is introduced by a long and hilarious farce, where Mak steals a sheep, and his wife pretends that it is her newly born infant—this at the same moment that the "lamb of God" is being born in a similar setting. In the York play of Jesus' trial, Pilate toys with his wife openly in court to the amusement of the spectators before Jesus is led in. In the Towneley *Buffetting of Christ*, the tormentors vie

with each other for turns at their victim and even bring
Christ into the game by blindfolding Him and demand-
ing that He guess who scourged Him last. And the
pinmakers and painters of York make a farce out of
fitting the body of Jesus onto a cross that was carelessly
made the wrong size.

What do all these scenes have in common? T. McAlindon in an article on "Comedy and Terror in Middle
English Literature" shows how some of the most fully
realized characters in the miracle plays are devils who,
"alive with energy, mobility, and success," provide endless delight by inflicting pain. Most important, "their
delight turns work into a sport, and so they present Hell
to their victims as an unending, varied game." McAlindon points out the genius of the medieval playwright in
seizing on the combination of malice and play as the
most dramatic way to present evil, which is the breaking
of divine order, and of terror and jest as the most striking
way to evoke Hell, which is sheer chaos. But let us carry
his line of reasoning further. The devils, tormentors,
blasphemers, thieves, liars, shrews, murderers are the
most vital characters in the play. They are the only
people who seem to have any fun in life, who, in fact,
seem to be living at all. This point becomes more evident when we look at the innumerable depictions of the
Dance of Death, where the living persons appear dead
and the death figures are singing and dancing. Sinners
and demons may have turned the world upside down
and turned order into chaos, but they have also created
life. We see them not so much causing the chaos as
enjoying it.

We may now distinguish between two opposing archetypal fool or clown figures, even though they are often
blended in varying measures in the same literary character. The first, as we have seen, is best exemplified in
Socrates but was familiar enough in the Middle Ages

and the Renaissance to serve Erasmus and Shakespeare. This fool destroys conventional reality, shows life to be a game, and turns the world upside down—all to reassert the basic, rational purpose in the universe. The second kind of fool, who cavorts in the Feast of Fools, the *sottie* drama, and the miracle plays, also annihilates reality, turns life into a game and the world upside down—but his result is chaos. Both kinds of fools affirm through play the creative vitality of the human spirit, the first through the rediscovery of life's permanent and primal order, the second through the improvisation of orders that are temporary but infinitely various. The dying Socrates and the eternally damned devil are far more alive than their living interlocutors. Both escape the wrath of the God of Revelation, when he warns, "I would thou wert cold or hot. So then because thou art lukewarm, and neither cold nor hot, I will spue thee out of my mouth."

Whether one approves or disapproves of William Burroughs's *Naked Lunch*, there is little danger of its being served up lukewarm. The novel's acclamation at the 1962 Edinburgh Festival by Mary McCarthy and Norman Mailer was followed by a host of reviews that were solely cold or hot, and during the next year a long battle raged among the epistlers of the *Times Literary Supplement*. While readers of *Naked Lunch* are diminishing, the novel has been made a part of America's literary and cultural history by some of our best critics, and for good reason. For Burroughs attacked our society not so much as a satirist with the desire to reform, but, as Tony Tanner has shown in a brilliant discussion of Burroughs's works, to attack and destroy the foundations of Western culture. The power and vitality of *Naked Lunch*, his best novel, are due to its sheer destructiveness.

There is no need to investigate the apocryphal genesis,

to decide how much of the book was heroin hallucination and how much was edited by Burroughs and/or Allen Ginsberg. We can take the novel at face value. "The title," Burroughs insists, "means exactly what the words say: NAKED Lunch—a frozen moment when everyone sees what is on the end of every fork." Straight off, the narrator implies that this dope addict's picture, however obscene and eccentric, is his metaphor for the modern human condition. The implication is developed more explicitly when he describes the "pyramid of junk," where from the highest entrepreneur to the lowest pusher and from the lowest pusher to the most degenerate addict one level feeds on the level below—and "it is no accident that junk higher-ups are always fat and the addict on the street is always thin." The principles upon which this pyramid is built could easily apply to the whole Western and Westernized world's scheme of economic and social values: "1—Never give anything away for nothing. 2—Never give more than you have to give (always catch the buyer hungry and always make him wait). 3—Always take everything back if you possibly can."

But as we read on in the novel two questions arise: Where, in relation to the world he describes, does the narrator stand? What is his attitude toward the naked lunch? For at first we are listening to a man who has escaped from the addict's world, and who is going to describe it with unsparing accuracy; his tone is objective to the point of appearing scientific, and he is clearly didactic. But suddenly we find that the narrator is no longer standing apart from the addict's world but describing what he sees from within. He has shifted into a new gear—his style is jazzy, his diction argot, his posture involved, his attitude quivering between joy and outrage. Throughout the novel we are uncertain whether drug addiction is the living death he claims it to be when he is objective, or whether with all its repulsiveness it is not a vital and creative response to the terrifying emptiness of modern life.

The novel's ambiguity could easily be dismissed as a kind of formless and arrogantly uncritical rebellion of the beatnik tribe. But this novel continues to be disturbing, to coerce us to look again at what is on the end of our forks, and I think this is in great part due to a contradiction not bridged by the fine irony to which we have become accustomed in the modern novel.

The ambiguity of *Naked Lunch* is established in the introduction, which literally splits in two with scant transition when the narrator concludes his "Deposition" and begins "speaking *Personally*." This formal split results from the narrator's schizophrenic point of view, which can be compared instructively to the double perspective employed by Dickens, Dostoyevsky, Kafka, and O'Connor. In the first part, Burroughs's narrator is a converted drug addict addressing society—a square addressing squares. But in the second part, he alienates the average reader and excludes the squares just as Genet excludes the white spectators whom he insists be present at performances of *The Blacks*. Now the narrator is an insider addressing insiders, and he ends his introduction with the call "Paregoric Babies of the World Unite" and with a sardonic admonition to the young initiate.

The novel can be said to take off from an initial scene in the Kafkaesque Reconditioning Center, which Dr. Benway has established in Freeland. The doctor learns that the electronic brain has gone berserk playing six-dimensional chess with the technician, and it has released all the inmates. From the rooftop Benway and the narrator view the result—an apocalyptic vision of the most fantastic kinds of perversion and sadism. And the scene is shaped in the form of a tall tale, except that the terrifying and repulsive overtones often obscure the comedy. At one point the narrator stops and turns to us, "Gentle reader, the ugliness of that spectacle buggers description. . . . I fain would spare you this, but my pen hath its will like the Ancient Mariner." This last reference is more than a sly wink at the Great Romantic Junkie, for Burroughs's narrator is the Modern Mariner, and the parallel is important. When the Ancient Mariner is converted he becomes a square; he discovers that the square world is beautiful and valuable, and he laments his earlier "Life-in-Death." The Modern Mariner is converted too, but his lament is ambivalent; the descriptions of his Life-in-Death are too lively.

The style of the whole book is schizophrenic, hovering between mock-scientific reporting and jazzlike improvisation. Burroughs's definitions are ingenious and convincing: the "smother party," which derives from "a rural English custom designed to eliminate aged and bedfast dependents"; "Bang-utot," which is a "condition . . . [occurring] in males of S.E. Asiatic extraction," who die dreaming that the penis has entered the body and killed them; the "Mugwump," a person who "has no liver, maintaining himself exclusive on sweets"; the "Latah," who at the snap of the fingers compulsively imitates one's every motion and has been known to injure himself trying to imitate the motions of several people at once. The small-scale inventiveness is developed to an extreme in the wildly sadistic and obscene improvisations that pervade the novel. And while the improvisations are destructive we must not ignore their creative dimension; they are disarming, in fact, just because they are destructive and creative simultaneously. For while the improvisations are obscene and perhaps the product of narcotic hallucination, the improvisor gathers his vital energy from renewed attacks on the middle-class bringers of death. He shapes his fantasia of sexual perversion from caricatures of the businessman, who is symbolically and literally responsible for the "pyramid of junk." And Burroughs's style, reminiscent of Henry Miller's, can best be described as comic and orgiastic, where new and short-lived forms of life are born out of the continual destruction of the old.

We can push Burroughs's antecedent even further back, to Walt Whitman, who also combined scientific and orgiastic styles, relentless catalogs and life-evoking rhythms. One effect of this combination in both writers is to create a sense of veracity and universality: when we finish *Naked Lunch* we feel that junk is as common as grass, and the feeling is reinforced by current hippie argot.

This comparison with Whitman is not meant to elevate Burroughs's achievements; it might even serve to measure his limitations. But, then, the differences are not only of genius but also of world view. The contradictions that Whitman and his transcendentalist predecessors so proudly embraced were rooted in an underlying order—every separate person, thing, artifact was an individuation of the Eternal Spirit. In Burroughs's world, however, the contradictions result from an essential and universal chaos. It may be a disguised platitude to say that in the last hundred years our sacred symbol has changed from grass to junk, but it is interesting to note how little the sacerdotal attitude has changed with it. Following the theory of Charles Walcutt's *American Literary Naturalism*, we might say that the naturalism and scientism in *Naked Lunch* spring from transcendentalist sources, from a sacred attitude toward the mundane. But when faith in eternal harmony is lost, when the common object is no longer a symbol for the heavenly essence, esthetic and organic order gives way to improvisation. When Burroughs fixes his attention on the lowest stratum of our society and its most repulsive activities, it is in part to protest that this is both the result and image of middle-class living, but it is also to transform it, as Whitman transformed his quotidian detail, into a life-invoking ritual. However, Whitman was prophetic and Burroughs is apocalyptic; Whitman sang about new beginnings, Burroughs shows a world bent on destruction. The ritual in *Naked Lunch* begins with destruction, and the evanescent new life will not be in the form of the old.

The true beginning for the narrator of *Naked Lunch* comes toward the end of the novel, when he shoots Hauser and O'Brien, the Narcotic Cops who had been the first to arrest him fifteen years earlier. After calling the Narcotics Bureau he discovers that there is no Hauser or O'Brien, that in the final step of his addiction he has been "occluded from space-time," "locked out," never again to have "a Key, a Point of Intersection." The implication here is twofold. First, the narrator's tale begins with an act of destruction. Second, the act is imaginative, since he is occluded from objective reality, although nonetheless destructive. The arch destroyer in *Naked Lunch* is the narrator, who destroys our familiar world with his imagination. One way he destroys it is through his schizophrenic point of view, for when he addresses us as a convert he draws us into his world, and when he speaks with the voice of the junkie he quickly sunders all connections with the world we know. The other way he destroys is through an improvisation that abrogates order and depends on building anew with each step. He is like the medieval rebels and demons—Cain and the tormentors of the miracle plays, the fools of the *sottie* drama, the leaders of the Dance of Death—who thrived on destruction and perversely affirmed life by improvising in an orderless world.

Since *Naked Lunch* ritualistically destroys our habitual ways of seeing and judging, we may seem to lack a basis for criticism. Fortunately this is not the case. Bur-

roughs had both courage and ingenuity in presenting us
with the devil's view of the world, and his book is far
more honest than Mailer's *American Dream*, which
reaches toward the same end. Still, Burroughs has let us
down. We can think back to the vitality of the Wake-
field Cain, we can remember the sportiveness of the
York tormentors, we can recall the *sottie* fools who
ended their plays by destroying their whole flimsy world,
and the innumerable Death figures who were so mali-
ciously alive as they led Society through its dance. Burroughs's improvisations lack the sharpness, the individu-
ality, the variety of his medieval predecessors. And while
it would be easy to blame this on the dullness of modern
living or of the narcotic's escape, I rather think it is due
to his failure to fully live up to his role as destroyer, to
fully enjoy the act of destruction, to embrace contradiction instead of ambivalence—to accept the enormous
strain of improvising in the void.

In contrast to Burroughs, Vladimir Nabokov accepts
all the dangers and exhilarates the reader with his gleeful
and prolific destructiveness. In Robert Hughes's excellent film study of Nabokov, Nabokov describes the "first
thrill of diabolical pleasure that you have in finding, in
discovering that you have somehow cheated creation by
creating something yourself." The diabolical pleasure in
Lolita might also have resulted from the unique quality
of his creation. In this novel he leads us to an unexpected vantage, which causes us to see a tawdry and stale
world in vivid and vital detail. But he continually destroys this world through satire, parody, obvious literary
devices, and radical shifts in perspective.

Diana Butler points out the relationship between
Humbert Humbert's passion for nymphets and Nabokov's own passion for butterflies. Although she dimin-
ishes the novel by treating it as a game or mystery which
can be solved by the literary sleuth trained in symbol

hunting, she does help us understand the singular quality of Humbert's world. For Lolita's peculiar attraction, Humbert's thrills of discovery, and his feelings of horror and guilt at the inevitable destruction are all communicated through the implicit and pervasive metaphor of Lolita the prize butterfly. Alfred Appel, Jr., puts the point in its proper perspective and develops its more important implications.

Just as the nymph undergoes a metamorphosis in becoming the butterfly, so everything in *Lolita* is constantly in the process of metamorphosis, including the novel itself—a set of "notes" being compiled by an imprisoned man during a fifty-six day period for possible use at his trial, emerging as a book after his death, and then only after it has passed through yet another stage, the nominal "editorship" of John Ray, Jr. As Lolita turns from a girl into a woman, so Humbert's lust becomes love, his sense of a "safely solipsized" Lolita (p. 62) now replaced by his awareness that she was his "own creation" with "no will, no consciousness—indeed, no life of her own" (p. 64), that he did not know her (p. 286), and that their sexual intimacy only isolated him more completely from the helpless girl. These "metamorphoses" enable Humbert to transform a "crime" into a redeeming work of art, and the reader has watched the chrysalis come to life.

Mr. Appel's essay on *Lolita* is sensitive, erudite, and thorough; it is perhaps the most enlightening analysis of the novel. But the price of this kind of analysis is to scale down the novel's larger effects and dominant movements. The metaphor of the butterfly's metamorphosis is perfect, except that with its continual focus on the butterfly at the end of the process, it tends to obscure the stages of destruction. Humbert Humbert acknowledges, "I knew I had fallen in love with Lolita forever; but I also knew she would not be forever Lolita. She would be thirteen on January 1. In two years or so she would cease being a nymphet and would turn into a 'young girl,' and then, into a 'college girl'—that horror of horrors. The word 'forever' referred only to my own passion, to the eternal Lolita as reflected in my blood. The Lolita whose iliac crests had not yet flared, the Lolita that today I could touch and smell and hear and see, the Lolita of the strident voice and the rich brown hair—of the bangs and the swirls at the sides and the curls at the back, and the sticky hot neck, and the vulgar vocabulary—'revolting,' 'super,' 'luscious,' 'goon,' 'drip'—*that* Lolita, *my* Lolita, poor Catullus would lose forever." Lolita is as transient as a butterfly; Nabokov's accomplishment is in preserving her not in a "well-wrought urn" but in a form that maximizes the transiency, that is composed of continually shifting planes and perspectives, that ends with the reader not in possession of the esthetic object but possessed by it, drawn completely within it, so that at the moment of the novel's conclusion he is looking at his everyday world through the author's shifting lenses. Nabokov accomplishes this through a joyful destructiveness that takes two major forms—the first is endless multiplication, the second continual forward movement.

Lolita, light of my life, fire of my loins. My sin, my soul. Lo-lee-ta: the tip of the tongue taking a trip of three steps down the palate to tap, at three, on the teeth. Lo. Lee. Ta.

She was Lo, plain Lo, in the morning, standing four feet ten in one sock. She was Lola in slacks. She was Dolly at school. She was Dolores on the dotted line. But in my arms she was always Lolita.

In the novel's opening paragraphs we are given a fine example of Nabokov's style in *Lolita*. It is perhaps best characterized by its repetitive variation, its ability—through rhythm, sound patterns, puns, precision—to cause us to see an image in multiple flashes. The multiplicity is increased by relating Lolita to Humbert's first love, Annabel, and to the innumerable nymphets in literary history. And it is increased even more by the innumerable variations of the same scene of love-struck Humbert courting the tough-minded and tough-hearted Lolita. The four-page catalog of "Sunset Motels, U-Beam Cottages, Hillcrest Courts, Pine View Courts, Mountain View Courts, Skyline Courts, Park Plaza Courts, Green Acres Courts, Mac's Courts" is one of the most incisive evocations of the modern American landscape; but it is also a dramatic means to convey the multiple and identical scenes that took place over the period of a year and over the expanse of three thousand miles.

Still another way that Nabokov effects an experience of multiplicity is through the device of "the double." Critics have mentioned Nabokov's debt to Stevenson, Poe, Gogol, and Dostoyevsky; but they have failed to note that Nabokov does not follow his predecessors in using the double to explore psychic dimensions of a main character's personality. Clare Quilty, the writer, the man of the stage, the debauchee, the driver of an Aztec Red Convertible, is not a projection of the hero; there is no need for a projection in this full confession. Closer to Faulkner's Lucas Brown and O'Connor's Enoch Emery than to Dostoyevsky's Rogozhin, Clare Quilty is a parody and a comic repetition of Humbert Humbert. He mocks the hero, he arouses fresh sympathy for the hero—and he also conveys the impression that Humbert is not unique but one of many. The world is full of nymphets, and nympholepts as well.

The result of Nabokov's tricks of style, structure, and characterization is that we are led through a series of freshly evoked and quickly shattered experiences, which are nearly identical, and which take place in a world of nearly identical backdrops. Through what is in part a deliberate parody of Proust, Nabokov destroys our preconceptions of time and space. As we think back we almost feel as if time were composed of the same moment being repeated over and over, and as if space were pieced together from identical motelscapes.

This is not a complete description of our response, for the novel depends greatly on its continuing forward movement through both time and space. We are fascinated by what John Hollander calls Nabokov's "verbal diddle," we are affected by the multiplicity, we become lost in the intricate labyrinths, we are led on by the style, which, as Nabokov says of Gogol, follows "the dream road of his superhuman imagination"—but our most immediate concern is what happens next to Humbert Humbert. Will Humbert make contact with Lolita? How will he take care of Charlotte? What will happen when he arrives at Lolita's camp? When will he seduce his nymphet? Will he get caught by the police? Will the red convertible catch up? Will he find his runaway love? Will he get Quilty? If the first main dimension of the novel's structure is endless multiplication, the second is continual forward movement. The multiplication works at cross purposes to the forward movement but does not impede it. Rather, it creates an eccentric rhythm very much like that which Nabokov attributes to Gogol's "Overcoat": "a combination of two movements: a jerk and a glide. Imagine a trapdoor that opens under your feet with absurd suddenness, and a lyrical gust that sweeps you up and then lets you fall with a bump into the next traphole."

Nabokov's eccentric rhythm achieves its climax in the meeting of the doubles. This is the obligatory scene, demanded by the novel's continuing forward movement, and yet, after the scene with Dolly Schiller which eliminates Humbert's motivation, wholly gratuitous. Humbert fires into the thick pink rug. Quilty continues his banter until in the midst of a banal question he throws himself on the avenging gunman. "We rolled all over the floor, in each other's arms, like two huge helpless children. He was naked and goatish under his robe, and I felt suffocated as he rolled over me. I rolled over him. We rolled over me. They rolled over him. We rolled over us." Humbert's second shot sends Quilty into the music room, his fingers wiggling in the air, his rump heaving rapidly, where after a struggle over the door he sits down at the piano and plays "several atrociously vigorous, fundamentally hysterical, plangent chords, his jowels quivering, his spread hands tensely plunging, and his nostrils emitting the soundtrack snorts which had been absent from our fight." Struck in the side by Humbert's third bullet, Quilty rises from his chair "higher and higher, like old, gray, mad Nijinski, like Old Faithful . . . head thrown back in a howl, hand pressed to his brow, and with his other hand clutching his armpit as if stung by a hornet." Humbert chases him down the hall "with a kind of double, triple, kangaroo jump . . . bouncing up twice in his wake, and then bouncing between him and the front door in a ballet-like stiff bounce." "Suddenly dignified, and somewhat morose," Clare begins to ascend the broad stairs: "I fired three or four times in quick succession, wounding him at every blaze; and every time I did it to him, that horrible thing to him, his face would twitch in an absurd clownish manner, as if he were exaggerating the pain . . . [and] he would say under his breath, with a phoney British accent —all the while dreadfully twitching, shivering, smirking, but withal talking in a curiously detached and even amiable manner: 'Ah, that hurts, sir, enough! Ah, that hurts atrociously, my dear fellow. I pray you, desist.'" But the chase continues from room to room until Humbert corners the "blood-spattered but still buoyant" Quilty in his bed and shoots him through the blanket at close range: "a big pink bubble with juvenile connotations formed on his lips, grew to the size of a toy balloon, and vanished."

Down below, Humbert joins a number of people enjoying Quilty's liquor, and announces that he has just killed their host. " 'Good for you,' said the florid fellow as he offered one of the drinks to the elder girl. 'Somebody ought to have done it long ago,' remarked the fat man." And more repartee and music until there is a noise on the stairs.

Quilty of all people had managed to crawl out onto the landing, and there we could see him, flapping and heaving, and then subsiding, forever this time, in a purple heap.

"Hurry up, Cue," said Tony with a laugh. "I believe, he's still—" He returned to the drawing room, music drowned the rest of the sentence.

We have been swept up and let fall with a bump into the final traphole. This scene, which is the climax of the novel, coming just a few pages before the end, momentarily destroys our recollection of Humbert's evocations of the nymphet, the delights of his tentative conquests, the perceptions of her special grace, the poignancy of his meeting with Dolly Schiller. After Humbert's total acceptance of Lolita's metamorphosis, there is no explaining his need for vengeance. The violent shift in perspective completely destroys the already shifting foundations of the novel; it causes us to doubt the confusing impressions we have built up from scratch, as it were, of the narrator. What are we to make of a world where perversity is the only form that love can take, where the Grotesque is the only form of beauty, where madness is the only form of sanity, where obsession is the only form of freedom, where destruction is the only form of living? And what are we to make of Humbert Humbert, the hero, the victim, the creator of this world? Is he the comic-pathetic Romantic, forever in search of the unattainable? Is he the true and tender lover of Lolita and Dolly Schiller? Is he the mad sadist, the avenger-killer of Clare Quilty?

The *sotie* drama would end, to quote Miss Welsford, with "the turbulent fighting of fools" bringing "a jerry-built new world tumbling about their ears." *Lolita* ends with the turbulent fighting of the foolish lover/narrator and his double, destroying another jerry-built new world. With his fertile and daring imagination Humbert Humbert made the ugly Lolita into a nymphet of singular beauty. He destroyed her life but also transformed her imaginatively—giving her far more value than she would have achieved on her own. In the end, he destroys his imaginative creation with the final violent shift in perspective. This final shift forces us to question not Humbert Humbert's grasp of reality but our own. Quilty dies, Dolly dies, Humbert dies, the novel is over; but like the *sotie* fools, and like the ghost of Gogol's Akaky Akakyevich, the narrator who has gleefully destroyed everything in sight continues to haunt us.

7

Harlequin
The Character of the Clown in Saul Bellow's *Henderson the Rain King* and John Hawkes's *Second Skin*

Three different archetypal clown figures have been presented in the last three chapters. The first is the buffoon, physically undignified but eternally resilient, incapable of foresight or prudence, single-minded and simple-minded, who in his naïve and unselfconscious way "breaks down the distinction . . . between folly and wisdom." The second, exemplified in Plato's Socrates and Erasmus' Folly, also destroys conventional reality but shows life to be a game and turns the world upside down to reassert the basic purpose in the universe. The third kind of clown, who cavorts in the Feast of Fools, the *sottie* drama, and the miracle plays, annihilates reality, turns life into a game and the world upside down — but his result is chaos.

There is still another archetypal clown figure, who will be the subject of the next two chapters — Harlequin. Animated by a spirit close to that of the medieval demon, he continually breaks the laws of society and nature — but not out of rebellion and not toward the end of gleeful destruction. Sharing the innocence and underlying shrewdness of Socrates and Folly, he does not reaffirm a primal order. Apparently simple-minded and naïve like the buffoon, he is acutely aware of his situation and of himself. Harlequin thrives in chaos but to build rather than to destroy. His creations are silly, precarious, evanescent; but they bring positive pleasure and are a source of positive values. The world Harlequin inhabits is as irrational and menacing as the one left us by the medieval demon or the *sottie* fool. Harlequin has no illusions about this world but nevertheless affirms the greatness of the human spirit that can, in the words of William Faulkner, "not merely endure . . . [but] prevail."

Harlequin is fully aware of his situation, his nature, and the potentialities of his role. Saul Bellow's *Henderson the Rain King* and John Hawkes's *Second Skin* are well suited to explore the modern manifestation of Harlequin, his situation, nature, and role; for Bellow's emphasis on social reality and Hawkes's focus on psychological reality are ideal complements. Both writers suggest that absurd warfare is the condition of life, and that soldiers are turned into clowns. Bellow pictures Henderson, who always had a "soldierly rather than a civilian temperament."

When I was in the Army and caught the crabs, I went to get some powder. But when I reported what I had, four medics grabbed me, right at the crossroads, in the open they stripped me naked and they soaped and lathered me and shaved every hair from my body, back and front, armpits, pubic hair, mustache, eyebrows, and all. This was right near the waterfront at Salerno. Trucks filled with troops were passing, and fishermen and paisanos and kids and girls and women were looking on. The GIs were cheering and laughing and the paisans laughed, the whole coast laughed, and even I was laughing as I tried to kill all four. They ran away and left me bald and shivering, ugly, naked, prickling between the legs and under the arms, raging, laughing, and swearing revenge. These are things a man never forgets and afterward truly values. That beautiful sky, and the mad itch and the razors; and the Mediterranean, which is the cradle of man-

kind; the towering softness of the air; the sinking softness of
the water, where Ulysses got lost, where he, too, was naked as
the sirens sang.

Second Skin is the "naked history" of a fat, bald,
fifty-nine-year-old ex-skipper of a small naval vessel, who
undergoes a series of physical indignities and psychic
outrages. They begin with the suicide of the Skipper's
father, an undertaker, who shoots himself in a lavatory
while, outside the locked door, his young son tries to
distract him by playing Brahms on a cello. The father's
suicide is a signal, an omen. And it is with a mixture of
guilt, foreboding, and latent incestuous love that the
Skipper accompanies his daughter, Cassandra, on her
honeymoon trip in an old Packard loaded with black-
market tires; holds tight to her hand on a dark desert as
three soldiers strip, bury their gear, and then, naked
except for their steel helmets, take turns kissing her;
chaperones her at a high-school dance on their cold
Atlantic island where he is tricked into the belly-bump-
ing contest as she goes off with Red, Bub, and Jomo; and
escorts her aboard the *Peter Poor* where he is forced
below while Red makes love to her on the deck and the
boat heads for the rocks. Wraithlike and passive Cassandra is drawn from him until finally there is the drag race
on the moonlit beach as the Skipper tries to save her
from Jomo. No lights, no muffler, no windshield, accompanied by Miranda with her skirt billowing and her long
black hair stinging his eyes, the fat, bald Skipper drives
desperately, skillfully, up and down the rock-strewn
beach, forces his antagonist into the sea, and leaps to his
daughter's rescue—only to find that it is a decoy, that it
is Bub wearing Jomo's baseball cap. And so there is one
more race. Near exhaustion, the Skipper plunges through
the deep sand to the lighthouse, climbs the steel stairs,
and reaches the top to find a neat pile of his daughter's

clothing. The chase is over. Cassandra is down below on the sharp rocks.

Described with detachment, terror, parody, and slapstick, each outrage contains abortive love and frustrated heroism. The central outrage in the novel takes place during the war, aboard the U.S.S. *Starfish*, when a youth named Tremlow inspires the crew to mutiny by dancing in a grass skirt and violates the Skipper over a water keg. Throughout the novel Tremlow's name is continually recalled, as are the main images of the mutiny; for instance, the steel ladder the Skipper climbs to the pilothouse becomes the ladder he is carried down on the *Peter Poor* and the steel stairs of the lighthouse. The emphasis on the mutiny suggests that the senseless experience of the war was responsible for the violence, the perversion, the frustration, and the absurdity of the Skipper's world. It is the war that the father signals with his suicide shot, and that is symbolized by the black-market tires on Cassandra's honeymoon and the soldiers on the desert. It is the war's absurdity that is dramatized when the Skipper finds his son-in-law killed during a homosexual affair, on the day the fighting ends. It is the war's echo that we hear as Miranda listens to the "Horst Wessel," snips off the baby's rubber nipples with kitchen shears, and conspires in Cassandra's destruction. The war is not even forgotten in the lyric pastoral scenes on the last, tropic island, where the Skipper—still wearing his old naval cap and sneakers—has become an artificial inseminator and lover of the dark-skinned Catalina Kate.

Not only is war seen as the condition of life, but death is at the center of the worlds of both *Henderson the Rain King* and *Second Skin*. The plot of Bellow's novel moves to this center through stages of preparation, with the ritual destruction of the frogs among the peaceful Arnewi and the ritual moving of the rain god among the warlike Wariri, the intellectual exercises with Dahfu, and the physical exercises with the lion. And the threat of death changes from comic to tragic: first the King will be killed if he fails to satisfy every wife in his large harem; then the King, having become Henderson's best friend, is killed trying to capture a lion. This is the most moving scene in the novel, where Henderson is portrayed with the deepest sympathy and where his self-sacrifice lacks any comic overtone.

"King Dahfu!" I yelled out.

He was falling. Block and pully smashed down on the stone before the fleeing beaters. The king had fallen onto the lion. I saw the convulsion of the animal's hindquarters. The claws tore. Instantly there came blood, before the king could throw himself over. I now hung from the edge of the platform by my fingers, hung and then fell, shouting as I went. I wish this had been the eternal pit. The king had rolled himself from the lion. I pulled him farther away. Through the torn clothing his blood sprang out.

"Oh, King! My friend!" I covered up my face.

Death is more obviously at the center of Hawkes's world. The Skipper is haunted by the suicide or the potential suicide of each member of his family. The plot of the novel, although fractured in its presentation, moves from the death of Skipper's father to the mutiny on the *Starfish* to the death of Cassandra on the cold Atlantic island to a final celebration of birth in a tropic cemetery. "We melted wax and stuck candles everywhere we could on the dark stone, I jammed lighted candles among the weeds in the center of that listing shape. The little flames were popping up all over the grave and suddenly the unknown soul was lighting up Sonny's smile and mine and Kate's, was glowing in Kate's eyes and in the soft sweat on her brow."

There is a "heart of darkness," then, in the worlds of both *Henderson the Rain King* and *Second Skin;* but neither Henderson nor the Skipper is allowed to face it in the manner of Kurtz or Marlow. For the worlds of Bellow and Hawkes are not like Conrad's; and Jan Kott's comparison of the Grotesque world to the fun-house barrel of laughs is just as relevant here as it was in the works discussed above. But unlike the earlier heroes, Henderson and Skipper accept their roles as clown and their own foolishness with complete awareness. They are aware that war is the condition of life, that there is a heart of darkness which is all the more terrifying because it precludes the heroic posture. Moreover, they are aware of their own natures and of their potentials in the roles of clown. For this reason we can place them in the tradition of Harlequin.

The nature of the clown is best described by Enid Welsford, who concludes her study by illuminating the twofold human contradiction that he epitomizes.

In the first place we are creatures of the earth, propagating our species like other animals, in need of food, clothing and shelter and of the money that procures them. Yet if we need money, are we so wholly creatures of the earth? If we need to cover our nakedness by material clothes or spiritual ideals, are we so like the other animals? This incongruity is exploited by the Fool.

. . . .

But if man is not wholly of the earth, he is surely wholly of the world. He makes plans, legal codes, invents scientific methods and social systems by means of which he procures that material well-being which the animals gain in a less roundabout manner. Pitted against Leviathan, against the system that his group has created, the individual is almost as helpless as he is when pitted against the laws of Nature— and here, too, there is an inner contradiction. The normal man wills the existence of Leviathan because it is essential to his self-preservation, but the normal man has also a latent, subconscious antagonism to Leviathan because it is always threatening to swallow him whole, it thwarts, opposes and limits him, both as a "natural" and as an original personality. Therefore, whenever the clown baffles the policeman, whenever the fool makes the sage look silly, whenever the acrobat defeats the machine, there is a sudden sense of pressure relieved, of a birth of new joy and freedom.

The clown's function is also described by Miss Welsford, when she points out that in contrast to the tragic hero his role is not central; "he usually stands apart from the main action of the play, having a tendency not to focus but to dissolve events."

Bellow's protagonist is a singular variation of the *miles gloriosus*, the braggart soldier of classical comedy—he is ineffectual but his bragging has a basis in fact, and he laughs at himself more than he is laughed at by others. He fights every outrage with enormous vigor and Pyrrhic success. He chooses impossible challenges and accepts impossible odds—he seeks the meaning of life in the largest and darkest continent, he wrestles with the strongest tribesman, he strives to relieve the Arnewi of their frogs and the Wariri of their drought, he tries to carry the spirit of primitive vitality back to civilization in the form of a lion cub. But Africa becomes the mirror of civilization and of his own past; success in physical combat leads to greater physical danger; the Arnewi's frogs are destroyed at the expense of their entire water supply; and the Wariri's drought is relieved as a preparation for the death of the good king Dahfu—and for the crowning of Henderson, which threatens death for him as well. Nevertheless each encounter is related with comic enthusiasm, and Henderson achieves a moral victory because his clownish "soldierly temperament" enables him to accept life, even embrace it—"I love the old bitch just the way she is and I like to think I am always prepared for even the very worst she has to show me. I am a true adorer of life, and if I can't reach as high as the face of it, I plant my kiss somewhere lower down."

Henderson is a direct descendent of Gargantua in his attitude toward life and in embodying the contradictions of man's animal and spiritual natures. In the opening pages he tells us, "At birth I weighed fourteen pounds, and it was a tough delivery. Then I grew up. Six feet four inches tall. Two hundred and thirty pounds. An enormous head, rugged, with hair like Persian lamb's fur. Suspicious eyes, usually narrowed. Blustering ways. A great nose. I was one of three children and the only survivor. It took all my father's charity to forgive me and I don't think he ever made it altogether." And it does not require a great stretch of the literary imagination to compare the quests of Gargantua and Pantagruel, which were stimulated by gigantic appetites—both natural and intellectual, or civilized—with that of Henderson. Bellow epitomizes this appetite in the pulsing call that comes to Henderson, *"I want, I want, I want!"*

Henderson's natural antagonism toward not one but two wives is in the tradition of what Henry Bamford Parkes called the "metamorphosis of Leatherstocking." Natty Bumpo's distrust of Judith, Huck's preference for Jim, the rejection of marriage by the Western hero, the Hemingway hero, the hero of the American detective story, all reflect a Rousseauian distrust of social institutions, which woman and marriage symbolize. Henderson is also like the heroes following from James Fenimore Cooper through Gary Cooper in demonstrating his pride in physical and technical skills and his preference for experience over book learning.

And yet, as Henry Bamford Parkes also emphasizes, the archetypal American hero rejects civilization but not its values. The Lone Ranger may thunder off into the sunset crying "Hiyo Silver" without even kissing the girl he has saved, but he came into town in the first place for the sole purpose of preserving social order. Natty Bumpo continually recites the Christian values he learned in the settlement in a tongue suited more for the Ladies Literary Society than for the Great American Woods, Huck becomes one of the most unconsciously acute critics of American social deterioration, Jake Barnes creates private rituals to preserve values that are lost to the modern world he lives in. And Bellow's Henderson can never really leave the civilized world of his hereditary and immediate past. Henderson's family has a record of public service. He had "great ancestors," ambassadors and statesmen, and "loony ones" as well. "One got himself mixed up in the Boxer Rebellion, believing he was an Oriental . . . one was carried away in a balloon while publicizing the suffrage movement." A cousin was awarded the Corona Italia medal for working two weeks without sleep in the rescue operations after a Sicilian earthquake. "One of the old Hendersons, although far from being a minister, used to preach to his neighbors, and he would call them by hitting a bell in his yard with a crowbar. They all had to come." It is just this public spirit that Henderson manifests, naturally and spontaneously, when he sees anyone in need of help. He delights in bringing the Arnewi Queen a plastic raincoat, even though the Arnewi's are in a period of severe drought. Without a thought to his own safety he blows up a cistern and hoists an enormous wooden goddess to rid the Arnewis of their frogs and to bring the Wariris the much needed rain.

Moreover, Henderson's great desire to escape his wife and family and pig farm and all the blunders of his past is countered by his desire to recollect them. Henderson never really leaves America or his past. His adventures in Africa are transmogrified by his singular urban idiom. We are made aware of his past not by artificial flashbacks but by the natural and necessary associations of a man whose past continues to live with him in the present. Even when Henderson reaches the farthest point in his journey away from civilization, and in his attempt to become a lion tremulously approaches the great beast, the scene is described in incongruous analogies, similies, turns of phrase, and focus on detail that turns the event from terrifying to parodic.

I came forward one step and I cannot deny that there lay over my consciousness the shadow of the cat I had attempted to shoot under the bridge table. There was little besides the king's arm that I could see. He kept beckoning and I took extremely small steps in my rubber-soled shoes. The snarls of the animal were now as sharp as thorns to me, and blind patches as big as silver dollars came and went before my eyes. Between these opaque interruptions I could see the body of the animal as it flowed back and forth before the opening— the calm, murderous face and clear eyes and the heavy feet. The king reached backward and touched me; he gathered my arm in his fingers and drew me to his side. He now held me in his arm. "King, what do you need me here for?" I said in a whisper. The lioness, in turning, then bumped into me and when I felt her I gave a sigh.

Henderson is a caricature of the American hero described by Parkes, but as a caricature he is much a part of the tradition which, we should remember, was fused with and animated by that of the tall tale. In *Henderson the Rain King*, Bellow synthesized the hero of the Cooper-tall-tale tradition with the hero of the clown tradition to explore the contradictions of man in modern society. The consummate expression of Henderson's contradictory nature is the image of the comic giant tramping through the African jungle in his T-shirt and jockey shorts. Henderson gives full recognition to his condition when, after King Dahfu's death, he expresses his loss and solitude, "All I had left in the way of clothing was shoes and helmet, T-shirt, and the jockey shorts, and I sat on the floor, where I bent over double and cried without limit." This may be viewed as a parody of the great recognition scene in *King Lear*, where the Shakespearean

Rain King comprehends his loss and solitude, and the fact that "unaccommodated man" is a "poor, bare, forked animal." Parody, as Hazlitt reminds us, is not always satiric or denigrating; often, as in this case, it derives from a painful understanding.

Besides recognizing man at his lowest extreme, both Lear, especially in his confrontation with Goneril and Regan, and Henderson, with his continual desire to improve situations and understand experience, recognize that man needs more than nature can provide. This is the need that raises man above the beast, stimulates him to create systems and institutions, one of which requires a king. Lear came to a tragic understanding of the contradictory depth and height of human nature, and, as Jan Kott suggests, Lear came to this understanding by being turned from King to Clown. Although Henderson's feelings are far less intense than Lear's, he comes to a comic understanding of the same contradiction, and with great pain, ironically by being turned from Clown to King.

Concerned with man in society Bellow exploits the contradictions of physical vulnerability. John Hawkes, on the other hand, works with a vulnerability that is psychological. Skipper follows more in the tradition of Oedipus than that of Lear, of Tristram Shandy than that of Gargantua and Pantagruel. Throughout the novel he is driven to save each member of his family and the image of himself as son and father, even at the cost of outrage and indignity. But he fails to save his father, mother, and wife; and his paternal overprotectiveness helps drive Cassandra to her suicide. What Hawkes suggests with his clear psychological and literary allusions is that Skipper is driven as well by a natural desire for his father's death and for a relationship with Cassandra that could only be achieved by the destruction of her as a daughter. Further, the outrage and indignity expose and lacerate his vulnerable psyche, but they also bring him the same natural and ambivalent satisfaction achieved by Dostoyevsky's Underground Man. They assuage his feelings of guilt, they bring him a substitute pleasure, they provide for his only possible expression of free will.

Soft and sensitive, Skipper is immeasurably vulnerable in a world whose past and present is irrational and violent. Like Henderson, and also following in the tradition of Harlequin, he is able to live in such a world by accepting his role as clown. Unlike Henderson his aggression cannot be expressed outwardly, for he is not by nature a *miles gloriosus* but an *eiron*, a self-deprecator in the tradition of classical comedy. He is capable of love, whether the dark love for his daughter and the mutineer Tremlow, or the natural love for his granddaughter, his Negro messboy, and his island mistress; and he is capable of courage. But he recounts his "naked history" with sufficient detachment to see himself as a "large and innocent Iphigenia betrayed on the beach" (by a father starting off a senseless war) and spared to love and fight and live in his hapless way. His power is unobtrusive; his mode of attack is an apparent helplessness or escape. Skipper wills, with at least one part of his psyche, the destruction of his father, his tie to the past, and of his daughter, his tie to the present. The destruction is accomplished by what is at the same time heroic gesture, clownish impotence, willful helplessness. The escape is an ever-present fantasy, a warm tropic island where he can establish a society and a family that is psychologically ideal, where all the polymorphous forms of love are given free reign, where violence is transmuted into play, grotesqueness into lyricism.

While the traditional clown stands apart from the action to dissolve it, Henderson and Skipper, like so many clowns in modern literature, stand at the center, and in two ways, as heroes and as narrators. Still, they retain the power to dissolve events. When the clown stood apart from the main action, there was a balance between his world and the world from which he stood apart—between appearance and reality, the ideal and the actual. The structure of the comic play can be developed with fantastic intricacies and convolutions just because of its essential equilibrium. But with the clown at the center of the action the equilibrium and balance are destroyed. Appearance and reality, the ideal and the actual blend and mix. Henderson, as *miles gloriosus*, has no *eiron* to expose him, as he would have had in a classical play; he exposes himself with his own comic descriptions. He pictures a foolish hero who is an intruder in Africa both as a civilized man in a primitive continent and as a primitive man among highly civilized people. His world is thoroughly dissolved. Appearance and reality, the ideal and the real are thoroughly mixed because Henderson, gigantically embracing the natural contradictions of man and the special contradictions of man in the modern world, stands in the center of his novel as hero. And also because he narrates his story with a singular idiom that blends elements of the urban and the primitive, the hero and the clown. The plot is a parody of the plot of quest. Henderson goes to Africa to seek the primitive, the past, and the exotic; he finds the civilized, the present, the familiar. That Bellow ends his novel with Henderson galloping over the arctic plain of Newfoundland is not an evasion as many critics believe. It emphasizes that the end is tentative, that the process of self-discovery will never end because the nature of the self is contradictory and the nature of reality is absurd. And the ending is the direct outcome of making the gigantic clown central to the main action.

Hawkes's clown also dissolves reality. An *eiron* with no *miles gloriosus* to expose, he strips *us* of our preconceptions and forces us to question our attitudes toward all of the characters, the world they inhabit, and finally the world we inhabit. And he accomplishes this through the style and structure of the story he narrates. A distinctive feature of all Hawkes's novels is the extraordinary landscape, which despite its dreamlike quality conveys a sharp impression of surfaces and local detail, and despite its strangeness is distinctly the world we know. His earlier works, which take place in settings as varied as Germany after the First and Second World Wars, the arid American West, provincial Italy, Graham Greene's England, achieve their power through a surrealist shifting. *Second Skin* achieves its power, and its far greater range of style, experience, and emotion through comic dissolution, through its central focus on the clownish hero/narrator.

The novel's kaleidoscopic structure is composed of three major patterns. The first pattern contains what we can call the present time. Here the Skipper attempts to save Cassandra in settings variously calculated to explore and reveal his psychic states: a sailor bar in San Francisco's Chinatown, a Mexican desert where AWOL soldiers crawl on their bellies through the darkness, and the island where "the black wind was rising off the iron flanks of the Atlantic." The second pattern contains the recollected past, running from the father's suicide in the bathroom to the mutiny aboard the U.S.S. *Starfish*. And the third pattern contains the imaginary future upon a "wandering island . . . unlocated in space and quite out of time." Here the Skipper makes love to the warm and dark-skinned Catalina Kate, and here he reigns as Artificial Inseminator of the Cows, leading Sonny, Big Bertha, Kate, and Sister Josie among "orchids hanging down from the naked Indian trees," and along the "sawtoothed ridge among the soft hibiscus and poisoned thorns and, yes, the hummingbirds, the little quick jewels of my destiny."

The three patterns serve to reveal the sensitive and

fertile mind of the hero. And the hero/narrator, the clown at the center of the novel's action, continually dissolves his narrative in such a way as to keep us aware of their interrelationship—of the fact that interrelationship is what the story is about.

Henderson reveals the contradictions of modern social reality; Skipper surfaces the contradictions of modern man's psychological reality. Bellow pictures man as part beast and part king; Hawkes reveals him as destroyer and creator. Bellow turns his heroic clown into a clownish king to transvalue the values of compassion, responsibility, and dignity. Hawkes takes us deep inside the psyche of a bald, fat, bumbling ex-skipper to transvalue the values of love and courage. In neither case is the transvaluation based on an underlying primal order, as it was with Flannery O'Connor. Rather it is based on a hard, clear view of a world that offers no ultimate stability, meaning, or source for these values, except what can come from man's existential will and choice. This situation is explored to its limits in three works where the hero does not merely accept but actively chooses the role of clown, and this is the subject of the next chapter.

8

Which Way Is Up?
Ralph Ellison's *Invisible Man*, Günter Grass's *Tin Drum*, and Samuel Beckett's Trilogy

Ernst Curtius traces one view of the world as madhouse, or "the world upside-down," back to a classical formula called "stringing together impossibilities." Archilochus, shocked by an eclipse of the sun in 648 B.C., imagined that if Zeus could darken the earth anything was possible —the beast of the field might eat the food of the dolphin. Like so many later writers, Archilochus pictures the world as totally chaotic, impelled by caprice, and unredeemable from within; but what is strikingly evident in his simple formulation is that, after the destruction of order, he affirms the new—and infinite, if temporary and precarious—possibilities that are available.

It is ironic, although understandable, that the existentialists who advanced the idea of absurdity failed to realize its comic dimension, for, as I am trying to show, the best images of the world as absurd have a partly comic basis. The character whose history is one of living in chaos is not Sisyphus, whom Camus described as a victorious tragic hero, but the clown who plays the role of madman. Santayana described him as a person who sees the world as grotesque, but instead of being moved to wisdom or sympathy is "excited, flushed, and challenged by an absurd spectacle." If we turn for a moment to the *commedia dell'arte*, where the clown, playing the role of Harlequin, achieved his fullest development, we will find a model for the character who links the three works I will discuss. Harlequin not only thrived in chaos, he was an arch destroyer of order; but he was not a rebel. When he stole a pie or seduced a rich man's wife or turned a somersault without spilling his wine glass, he transgressed social law and abrogated the laws of nature out of sheer indifference. However this was only one side of his character. As Allardyce Nicoll reminds us, he was also self-conscious, impertinent, and slyly aware of the humor in his role. His freedom and success were the result of an arduously acquired professional skill, and no one who has seen a successful acrobat, clown, or mime will deny that an awareness of this skill is part of the spectator's experience. Harlequin destroyed the world of everyday, and then by "stringing together impossibilities" tested the limits of his mental and physical powers. Although he was lovable, he was estranged from the audience by his mask and style, and by the fact that he was continually creating a private play within the play his audience was watching. Our complex feeling about Harlequin, and the successful clowns who have succeeded him, comes from our sense that his indifference is only part of the act—and from the frightening feeling that since he has destroyed reality, the act is all there is. As we move through the novels of Ellison, Grass, and Beckett, we will find that as readers we have less orientation, that the clowns discover more successful ways of destroying rational orders, and that in testing their limitations against new stresses they affirm a kind of human greatness.

The dominant rhythm of *Invisible Man* is established early in the novel, when we move from the white man's club to the Golden Day. The movement is from the local to the universal, from the rational to the nonrational. At the white man's club the nameless Negro hero has been invited to receive a scholarship to college, but first he is mixed into a group of Negro toughs and forced by the drunken, jeering town fathers to gaze at a naked blonde, fight a blindfold "battle royal," and grab for coins on an electrified rug. Here we see how he is forced into the role of the Negro stereotype, compelled to become a puppet by the white gods who manipulate him, denied his visibility—his identity—by the social forces of the American South. At the Golden Day, a roadhouse near the college, where a group of mad Negro veterans are taken once a week for a day of whiskey and women, the young man and the white trustee in his charge witness a chaotic orgy and a rebellion of the inmates against their giant attendant. With the references to the adult world and a world war, the hero's situation has been expanded. And injustice, with its rational explanations, has become malevolent caprice: now we see that he is made a "mechanical man" by an anonymous authority, which the mad doctor sums up in the third person plural pronoun.

The rhythm is reiterated in the movement from the South to the North. The young hero, echoing the phrases of Candide when leaving the Westphalian castle of his childhood, is expelled from his idyllic campus, the comparatively logical world of the South, the relatively simple life of the adolescent, into the chaotic world of the North. And in an interview for the *Paris Review* (republished in *Shadow and Act*) Ellison explains how he changed his style from naturalism to expressionism to reflect the changes in the hero's situation. From episode to episode, the movement from the white man's club to the Golden Day is repeated, climaxing in the seduction of Sibyl and the Harlem race riot. The seduction scene with Sibyl is a comic fulfillment of the ritual in the white man's club: well paid by the Brotherhood, the nameless hero finally gets his white woman, and his remarks, as he tries to evade the fanatic desires of the woman who only wants to be raped by a Negro, parody the lines of the battle royal.

This is the most purely comic scene in the novel, and it signals the most radical step in the hero's development. The first step in his development had been logical: to join the Brotherhood. He was to discover that he had made a blind mistake in believing that history was rational, and that human identity and fraternity could be achieved through its logic; but through this mistake he advanced beyond the stage where identity equaled Negro, and where history was limited to the record of his race. He was to gain perspective—comic perspective—first, when he was shocked by the death of a Brotherhood defector into wondering, "What if history was a gambler instead of a force in a laboratory experiment . . . not a reasonable citizen, but a madman full of paranoid guile"; then, when he was forced to become a clown in the madman's world. Trying to escape from Ras the Destroyer, the mad black nationalist leader, he donned the wide hat and green glasses of the zoot-suiter. Mistaken in his new guise for Rinehart, the chameleon-like racketeer-lover-minister, the hero marveled at the man who could assume such varied roles. When he looked at the world through his green glasses and saw the dark, "merging fluidity of forms," he realized that this was the way Rinehart must have seen life—full of possibilities and "without boundaries." Now he recognized that the world was a madhouse, chaotic and threatening, but because there were no boundaries and no order there were infinite possibilities for improvising. Seen through Rinehart's green glasses the world became comic, and therefore capable of affirmation.

Invisible Man has learned to renounce views of life based, first, on the history of his race, then, on the history of mankind—both rational orders that assured him of a stable identity. His most radical step is from the rational and serious to the nonrational and comic; and Ellison tells us that this step is accentuated by a shift to surrealism. Now the nameless hero accepts the role of Rinehart to gain as mistress a spy in the Brotherhood hierarchy, and the ensuing scene is full of mistaken identity, slapstick pantomime, and freewheeling satire. The comedy in the scene with Sibyl is not only a reflection of the hero's new world, it provides sufficient confusion to prepare him for his full freedom. Rinehart, like the *sottie* fools and the demons of the miracle plays, exploits the possibilities of a chaotic world—and also contributes to its destructiveness. The hero's final step is a rejection of Rinehart. Having satisfied his lust for the drunken Sibyl with a comic message written in lipstick on her belly, he is suddenly called to Harlem, where a riot has started. Now his first thought is to erase the message and get Sibyl home safely.

The Harlem race riot is a more bitter and hilarious version of the mad orgy and revolt in the Golden Day. But while the early scene was irrational, it was placed within what Ellison would call the naturalistic context of the South, with rational points of reference in the logic of the young boy's life, and the explainable motives of the white citizens, the Negro college president, the Northern trustee. The picture of the Harlem race riot, however, is a pure "stringing together of impossibilities," for the context of the North is irrational. In the description of the looting we see one old woman struggling bowlegged beneath half a cow, and we hear another demand that her husband get only Wilson's bacon. Figures pass in stolen wigs and dress coats, carrying dummy rifles. A huge woman sits atop a milk wagon "like a tipsy fat lady in a circus parade" and ladles out free beer. A man wearing three hats and several pairs of suspenders leads a group to burn down their rat-infested tenement, ignoring the pleas of a woman about to give birth.

Blonde mannikins hang from lampposts. Ras the Destroyer, dressed as an Abyssinian chieftain and riding a black charger that had been used the day before to pull a vegetable cart, throws spears at the police.

The hero, running for his life, falls into a coal cellar. In the dark he can recognize that the nightmare madhouse is reality, and that the joke of the human condition is man's invisibility: the unique self cannot be seen. Now we understand that the novel has been a parody of the *Bildungsroman*, that the progress of the hero toward rational maturity has been just the reverse in this upside-down world. And now the hero can renounce all signs of identity, accept his absurd situation, and prepare to return to the world of light.

There are two problems in this unusual novel. First, how to develop a hero who until the very end lacks a personality. Second, how to make the final affirmation convincing and concrete. But these are only problems if we fail to distinguish narrator from hero. For although they are the same person, the narrator's point of view is established at the end of his adventures when he achieves his comic perspective, and the changes in style reflect the narrator's distance from his earlier self. This distance is not established in the first-person narrations of Bellow and Hawkes, for the relationship of perspectives is not their subject. If Ellison's hero is shallow, the voice of his narrator is fully developed. And if, as Irving Howe complains, Ellison cannot specify the possibilities his hero would find above ground, the narrator does discover and explore a rich range of possibilities in recounting, or, as Earl Rovit has suggested, improvising, the story of his life from the viewpoint of his final nonrational realization. In describing a world that the existentialists had grimly termed absurd, Ellison established a comic posture. He has shown that when both the blind and the rebellious are turned to puppets by the third-person plural pronoun, one way to maintain independence and integrity is to *play* the role of puppet, that is to choose the role of clown. In the role of clown the narrator strings together the impossibilities of his past life.

Our understanding of both Ralph Ellison's *Invisible Man* and Günter Grass's *Tin Drum* depends on a constant awareness of the narrative point of view. Ellison's prologue and epilogue signal the radical difference between the narrator and his younger self. Grass not only establishes his highly problematic viewpoint in the opening paragraph, he constantly reminds us that Oskar is narrating his story from a bed in a mental hospital. Despite certain important similarities, *The Tin Drum* can be said to begin where *Invisible Man* left off. For while Ellison describes a mad world, and while we are made to see the folly and blindness of the young hero who tries to be rational, we are never made to doubt the narrator's observations. Grass, on the other hand, begins his novel by calling the reliability of his narrator to question, thereby totally denying us a secure vantage point.

In the opening paragraph Oskar addresses the reader: "Granted: I am an inmate of a mental hospital; my keeper is watching me, he never lets me out of his sight." Oskar is shown to be highly intelligent and perceptive, but the only fact we can start with is that he is in a mental hospital. There is no use questioning this fact, for even if he is inventing or imagining it, we still have the problem of madness as a starting point. We know, too, that the narrator has been judged mad by society, and/or (again it amounts to the same thing) the narrator judges society mad. Since the novel's point of view is completely that of a man considered mad, there is no way to establish an objective referent by which to judge or measure his reliability. The situation is complicated even further with the introduction of Oskar's keeper,

Bruno. We might take Bruno to be an objective referent: he is employed by society, he keeps constant watch
on Oskar, he even writes a chapter of Oskar's memoirs
when Oskar has strained his fingers—and this chapter
with its factual and objective style focuses on Oskar the
patient rather than the Oskar of the memoirs. Of course,
given the convention established in the opening of the
novel, we have no way of knowing that Oskar did not
write the Bruno chapter himself. Furthermore, although
Bruno keeps constant watch through the peephole, we
are told in the first paragraph that "my keeper's eye is
the shade of brown that can never see through a blue-
eyed type like me. So you see, my keeper can't be an
enemy." There is a conflict between Oskar and Bruno,
which greatly increases the complexity of the novel, but
the main conflict is between those inside the hospital
(both the keeper and the patient) and those outside.
"Once a week a visiting day breaks in on the stillness
that I plait between the white metal bars [of his bed].
This is the time for the people who want to save me,
whom it amuses to love me, who try to esteem and
respect themselves, to get to know themselves through
me."

Oskar, who has been plaiting stillness on the white
bars of his hospital bed, decides to plait his memories on
the blank space of the virgin paper he requires of his
keeper. Both Oskar and Bruno are artists. Bruno fashions
"knot constructions" out of pieces of string from the
visitors' presents; after disentangling the string he "works
them up into elaborate contorted spooks." While his
keeper improvises on bits of leftover string, Oskar disen-
tangles the bits and pieces of his past by improvising on
his drum, and then works them up, or records his improvisations on the virgin paper. My use of the term
"improvisation" might be questioned. But we should
remember: first, that we have no way of judging whether

he is recollecting or inventing; second, that he admits his memories may be inaccurate and that only his drum, when "handled adroitly and patiently," will evoke the details of his past; and third, that given the madhouse convention where the world is turned upside down, the irrational and imagined will be at least as telling as the rational and reported. Oskar takes as his "norm and standard . . . goal attained at last" the white enameled hospital bed, for it is the very opposite of the world created by the Black Witch, whom, remember, he deliberately evokes at the end of the novel and connects with all the events that took place in the world outside. All we *know* about Oskar's world is that there is an opposition between the world of the Black Witch and the world of the white bed, but we have no way of judging or measuring the nature of this opposition. The ever-shifting foundation of the novel makes its world even madder than Ellison's. Seducing the reader into a world of nearly recognizable symbols and half-completed allegories, Grass denies him a map or a guide. Further, he applies far more stress on the clown who improvises in its abyss. But he can also create a far more complex picture of ambivalent human relationships and intricate moral problems. And ironically, he can add heroic stature to the misshapen dwarf who is able to envision such a world.

Grass has written a modern *Divine Comedy*. But while the reader of *The Divine Comedy* is guided by Dante, who in turn is guided by Virgil, Matilda, Beatrice, and Bernard, the reader of *The Tin Drum* is never sure where Oskar is taking him or has taken him, and Oskar himself has to improvise his own paths. While Dante's cosmos is rational and orderly, Grass's is irrational and shifting. While the center of Dante's Hell, the antipode of love and life, is frozen and inert, Grass's hell has no center and is the source of destructive energy.

In Dante's world we would have been able to judge whether Oskar, playing with the "watering can" of the plaster boy Jesus and teaching him to drum, was acting the role of naïve saint or arch blasphemer. In Dante's world we would have been able to know whether his action was responsible for the symbolic descent of Christ into Hell, which follows in the surrealistic next chapter, called "Good Friday Fare," or whether he was exposing a "pseudo Jesus" and a false religion—just as the fisherman, saying "s'pose we take a look," exposes the horsehead stuffed with squirming eels. In Dante's world we would have been able to understand the relation between these events and his mother's gorging herself to death on fish, and whether this, which signals the acceleration of Nazi activity, was an act of repentance or an act of irresponsible gluttony no different from that of the Nazis. Furthermore, we would be able to judge whether Oskar was innocent or responsible for the deaths of his mother and two fathers. In short, we would be able to answer those who criticize Grass's neutrality and indecision; but we would then be evading the full terror of Grass's hell, which allows no maps or guides, and we would be ignoring the compassion of a writer who is able to see his hell so clearly—a compassion Dante never had.

At the end of the novel Oskar irrationally chooses to accept the guilt for a murder of which he was not only innocent but the inventor; then he flees. On the train he wonders what he should fear, for "what is worth running away from if all the police can wring from you is fresh, early-morning laughter?" And then he improvises a fear and imagines a song taking shape from the rhythm of the wheels, "Where's the Witch, black as pitch? Here's the black, wicked Witch." And in the last pages of the novel we see him transform the world he envisioned in his white hospital bed into the blackness of the Witch's creation. But just before he is captured by the Interpol (reminiscent of Ellison's "them" and Kafka's omniscient authorities) he describes his ascent from the metro station to the airport in an escalator. And now, his fear having been fully formed, he laughs and compares himself to "Dante on his way back from hell." Now we are faced with the explicit reference to *The Divine Comedy*, but what are we to make of it? Is the escalator Purgatory? Is the white mental hospital Heaven?

As usual, Grass's allegory is enigmatic. Further, he offers us no stable vantage point to determine whether Oskar is really going up or down, whether the hospital might not be more Purgatory or Hell itself. We must always remember that Oskar is mad or considered mad. And his release from the mental hospital, if it occurs, will be just as mad, for it will be determined not by an examination of the inmate but by some new *facts* about a crime the inmate invented. The total absurdity of Oskar's situation is confirmed by his response to the Interpol at the top of the escalator, "Ich bin Jesus." Oskar has likened the escalator not only to Dante's Purgatory but to the escalation and progress in Western Germany after the war (he considers all the economic possibilities now open to him) and hence to the whole Western idea of progress, grounded in the Christian eschatology, the scientific positivism, and the romantic evolutionism that had its climax in Hitler's Germany. Was Oskar going up or down?

We cannot know whether Oskar actually decided to stop growing, or if this story was improvised in his hospital bed. But whether it was a fact in his history or a fancy in his imagination, when he "refused to measure his shadow with theirs," Oskar not only stepped out of the adult world—he stepped out of all the ideological orders that shaped this world. Without the orders of God, Nature, or Science, there is nothing left but the madhouse.

All the writers discussed prior to this chapter employed the split perspective, but Ellison, Grass, and Beckett make this the subject of their novels. In *Invisible Man* we see the world from two perspectives, that of the hero and that of the narrator; we learn that the hero's rational view of the world, like the ordinary man's, is inadequate. But Ellison does provide us with a normal and stable referent from which we can measure the clown's departure. The novel is about the transition from normal blindness to existential vision. *The Tin Drum* lacks this transition; it starts with the nonrational, abnormal perspective of the clown. But Oskar does have an identity and a history, even if these have been improvised from his hospital bed. The novel's point of view might be ambiguous and from an objective standpoint unreliable, but it is single and identifiable. In Samuel Beckett's trilogy, *Molloy, Malone Dies,* and *The Unnamable,* not only is the narrator unreliable—he deliberately invents contradictions—he has neither identity nor history. In fact as we read through the stories of Molloy, Moran, Macmann, Mahood, Worm, we cannot possibly know who is the narrator, or whether the narrators are one or many. In a world of total relativity we cannot tell the storyteller from his story.

The story of A and C, in the beginning of *Molloy,* is a paradigm for the novel, in fact for the whole trilogy. Molloy, who tells us that he is writing his history from his dead mother's bed, admits that it is hard to tell himself from other people and that he may be inventing or embellishing what follows. A and C were slowly walking toward each other on a hard, white road. One was small and the other tall. "They looked alike, but no more than others do." They had left town separately and now the first was returning; it may have been either A or C since Molloy can't remember one from the other. They may have known each other; if not they certainly did after they met, stopped, exchanged a few words, and then continued in their separate directions. A (or possibly C), urbane, smoking a cigar, wearing sand shoes, leading a Pomeranian dog—but possibly none of these—returned to town. C (or possibly A), wearing a cocked hat and carrying a stout stick, innocent but fearful, went with uncertain steps through the lonely and treacherous hills. Molloy, camouflaged against a rock, observed.

As the novel continues, we find Molloy, impelled by some unknown desire, going in quest of his mother. Starting with his crutches and bicycle, he is reduced to his crutches alone, and after a number of treacherous experiences, including one where he meets and beats a charcoal burner, he is reduced to crawling and then rolling, until he ends motionless in a ditch. In the second part of the novel, Moran, a complacent bourgeois, is aroused from his sunny garden by Gaber, a messenger from Youdi, who sends him in search of Molloy. Moran, who is writing the story from his bed, tells us that Molloy (or Mollose) might be his invention or he might have found him ready-made in his head. In fact, there is no evidence that Molloy had any objective existence, since there were four Molloys: the one within Moran, Moran's caricature of the same, Gaber's Molloy, and Youdi's—whose Molloy would be the same as the obedient Gaber's except that Youdi changes his mind. Fully equipped and leading his son, Moran goes in search of Molloy. Eventually his son leads him, then abandons him. Finally Moran is poor, alone, and crippled. He meets a man with a stick, and then a dim man who resembles Moran and who is searching for the man with the stick, and he bashes in the head of the dim man. After an order from Gaber, he slowly and painfully returns to his now dilapidated home. Having started strong, well dressed, certain, satisfied, he ends looking and acting just like Molloy. Having begun his story in a

conventional manner, he concludes with a series of contradictions and sounds like Molloy.

When we finish the novel we wonder whether the
story was about Molloy telling his own story and telling
or inventing Moran's, or about Moran telling of his
conversion to Molloy, or about two characters who un-
derwent separate but similar experiences. In the next
novel, where Malone, unable to move from his bed,
improvises stories while waiting to die, we are led to
wonder if Molloy/Moran is telling a new story or if
Molloy/Moran was one of Malone's many inventions.
And when the Unnamable, ancient and limbless, kept in
a jar beneath a restaurant sign, tells us that Malone
passes before him "at doubtless regular intervals, unless
it is I who pass before him," the range of possibilities is
multiplied anew. All the possibilities can be reduced to
two outrageous alternatives: either there is a single narrator and all the characters are projections of his mind, or
there are many narrators, who, despite their similarity,
have no dramatized connection. If the first is true, then
Beckett's world is solipsistic, and nothing exists outside
the mind of a single character. If the second is true, then
his world is made up of a great number of isolated
characters, and no communication or knowledge is possible.

To return to the story of A and C, we are told that
there are two men approaching each other from different
directions, and they are being observed by the presump-
tive narrator. But if A and C and the narrator are the
same person, then the narrator cannot possibly be an
objective observer. And if A and C and the narrator are
different persons who undergo identical experiences,
then there is no way of telling one from the other, nor is
there any way of telling who is moving in what direction
or who is observing whom. Since in either case the reader
is denied a stable and objective observer, he has no way

of deciding between alternatives. The alternatives are contradictory, yet each accounts for all the evidence.

In his trilogy Beckett has confirmed *The Physicist's Conception of Nature*, where Werner Heisenberg explains how an objective view of reality is an oversimplification and a distortion, since there can be no objectivity. Not only is the observer's view of the phenomena limited by his position, it actually causes a disturbance in the phenomena he observes. Hence, the scientist must take into account both the fact and the position of his observations. And "method and object can no longer be separated." Further, it has been found that two mutually exclusive theories can be fully adequate for different experiments. And following Niels Bohr, who introduced "the concept of complementarity," the scientist has learned to live with these contradictions. But the scientist has an advantage, for he can limit himself to the particular end of a given experiment; his conclusions need only explain pragmatically a limited area of experience. In *Invisible Man* we had the young hero as a stable referent, in *The Tin Drum* we had a perhaps mad dwarf. But Beckett has taken us beyond the madhouse visions of Ellison and Grass in describing a world where there is no stable referent at all. He explores the frightening and exhilarating human consequences of Heisenberg's uncertainty principle.

In each book of the trilogy Beckett immerses us more and more deeply in the experience of uncertainty: he concludes with a parody of Descartes, who proved that since he doubted everything, it was at least certain that he, the doubter, existed. As in Kafka, man is compelled to identify himself and at the same time denied the possibility of doing so. But Beckett goes even further. He shows his characters compelled to speak, but he also shows that language either falsifies experience or is irrelevant to it. And since even to conceive oneself as a doubter is a verbal act, this conception is either false or irrelevant. The Unnamable demonstrates the fallacy of *cogito ergo sum;* Beckett denies his characters even the certainty of their existence. When we finish his trilogy, we come to understand that identity requires definition, requires that one discover the differentia between himself and the rest of the world. And in a truly absurd world, where there is neither causality nor order, finding the differentia is impossible—hence the comedy and hence the terror.

The most reliable image of Molloy should exist in the mind of Youdi, but Youdi changes his mind. Thus Beckett expresses the indifference and the irresponsibility of the central authority in his novel, the ruler, the Creator himself. But Beckett does not stop here, for this would at least suggest that Molloy could be differentiated from Youdi. When we finish the trilogy, we can look back and wonder whether Youdi might not be an invention of Gaber, or whether both might not be inventions of Molloy or Moran or the Unnamable or whoever is really telling the story.

In the next novel we find Macmann in an asylum. He develops a grotesque but nonetheless tender and deep relationship with Moll, his ancient and repulsive attendant. Moll wears a crucifix hanging from each earlobe, one for each of the criminals, and has the Cross of Christ carved on her single tooth, which wobbles precariously in her gums and is in constant danger of being swallowed or lost. Since by now we are immersed in Beckett's wildly relativistic universe, we see that from the vantage of Moll and Macmann, God is precariously balanced on the weak gums of a foolish old woman. From the narrator's vantage we see that Moll and Macmann are just as precariously balanced in life and just as much at the mercy of their creator(s); on the next page Malone considers the possibility of killing Moll off, and he finally does.

In *Malone Dies*, characters cannot be differentiated from their creators. In *The Unnamable* a character cannot be differentiated from the world. The Unnamable is a mere stump of human life who lives in a jar beneath a restaurant sign. At one time he had a sense of himself, for he could feel the sawdust pressing against him. But he has shrunken. "The sawdust no longer presses against my stumps, I don't know where I end." He feels enclosed, but with nothing touching him he cannot know if he is within or without. But the Unnamable not only lacks a physical differentia, he lacks a mental differentia as well. Like Descartes, he constantly questions and doubts, but unlike Descartes he cannot tell whether his questioning and doubting are stimulated from within or without. He is puzzled by "the thought of being indebted for . . . information to persons with whom I can never have been in contact." He tries to tell the story of Mahood, but it was Mahood who "told me stories about me . . . his voice continued to testify for me, as though woven into mine, preventing me from saying who I was." He tries to conceive of his relation to "them": they hope "that one day on my windpipe, or some other section of the conduit, a nice little abscess will form, with an idea inside."

In his jar, the Unnamable is totally dependent upon the proprietress of the restaurant, Marguerite or Madeleine, who changes his sawdust and throws a tarpaulin over his head in bad weather. She is considerate and tender, but she is also selfish and capricious. The Unnamable realizes that she is God in his universe, just as he also realizes that she needs him to fill up her void. Once again the hero is denied physical or mental differentia. The Unnamable is pictured at the lowest point of human existence. He is fully aware of the uncertainty in his world, and he is fully aware of his physical, psychological, and metaphysical vulnerability. Nevertheless he finds a way to assert himself. He ducks his head into the jar to hide from his mistress. And he forces her to fit a collar round his neck to keep him in sight. This comic action symbolizes the creative assertiveness of the Unnamable throughout the novel, when, reduced to the very threshold of human existence, he playfully explores every facet and ramification.

As the converted Moran explains, "when you can neither stand nor sit with comfort, you take refuge in the horizontal, like a child in its mother's lap. You explore it as never before and find it possessed of unsuspected delights. In short it becomes infinite." The further we get into Beckett's trilogy, the more helpless we find his characters and the more absurd and capricious their universe—whether objective or subjective. But the worse the situation, the greater the inventiveness and creative energy of the main character. The more terrifying the landscape, the more vital the clown. And here is Beckett's great humanistic affirmation. In all three works I have considered, we reach a point where we cannot tell progress from regression: Ellison parodies the form of the *Bildungsroman*, Grass mocks Dante's ascent from Hell, Beckett has the converted Moran announce his goal: "to be literally incapable of motion at last. . . . And mute into the bargain! And perhaps as deaf as a post! And who knows as blind as a bat! And as likely as not your memory a blank!" Molloy/Moran, Malone, the Unnamable achieve various degrees of success in reaching this goal. And from the narrator of *Invisible Man* to Oskar to the Unnamable, we have progressive denunciations of the Western ideal of progress, which has been expressed through its eschatological religion, its belief in evolution, and its faith in science. And we have progressive affirmations of madness to oppose the Western ideal of rationality.

Ironically one dimension of the humanist tradition, based on the exaltation of reason, has been denied in order to achieve a modern humanistic affirmation. But the human mind has not been denigrated by our best writers, for like Archilochus, in "stringing together impossibilities," they present the utmost challenge to the human imagination and intellect. The full nature of this challenge will be examined in the concluding chapter.

9

The Incarnate Word Was Never Known to Laugh

The content of Grotesque art, summarizes Wolfgang Kayser, has always consisted of monsters; animals like snakes, toads, spiders (those "nocturnal and creeping animals which inhabit realms apart from and inaccessible to man"); the bat, whose very name in German, *Fledermaus,* suggests the "unnatural fusion of organic realms"; plants with an ominous vitality; tools with a menacing life of their own; puppets; masks; madmen. Thus the Grotesque achieves its effect, of instilling "fear of life rather than fear of death," by crossing and fusing different realms of nature or realms of the natural and unnatural. Indeed the term "Grotesque" was initially applied to a style of painting, which consisted of bizarre combinations of natural and decorative forms. The fear of life is realized because the artist's creation is composed of familiar elements, and yet the categories we have developed for them no longer apply. We are drawn into a world that appears familiar, and then this world, and with it our basis for emotional and psychological security, is destroyed by an apparently arbitrary and certainly unfathomable shifting. Most importantly, the power that effects the shifting is obscured from our vision.

This Grotesque shifting is the subject of Dostoyevsky's *Idiot* and Kafka's "Metamorphosis." In these works we see two sensitive and compassionate men denied their humanity; we are held witness to the gratuitous transformation of the human into the subhuman or the nonhuman. The chief instrument used by Dostoyevsky and Kafka is a sudden mechanization of the scene: the compassionate Myshkin is transformed into a puppet; the sensitive Gregor, whose sensibility is heightened as we see him imprisoned in the body of an insect, is transformed into an irrelevant cartoon figure. The transformation, achieved by a formal reordering of the scene, denies us the possibility of locating the responsible power. Life in these works is terrifying because it is controlled by a power that is capricious and obscure.

Terror in *Great Expectations* and *The Trial* is achieved by showing human beings excluded from the human order. The threat, rather than being an obscure transcendent power, becomes an obscure power that is immanent. Meaning, purpose, direction are denied by an energy that takes the form of a pervasive "rebellion of means against ends." By a kind of Grotesque shifting that results in comic collisions, Dickens and Kafka achieve this effect. Characters collide as they discourse in private languages, objects senselessly assert themselves against each other and against men, bodies and parts of bodies assault one another. The result of these absurd collisions is that man feels himself an intruder in a world composed of infinite and infinitely different opposing forces. The theme of intrusion is reinforced by showing the sympathetic hero to be the *alazon*, the impostor and intruder of classical comedy. And the result is a travesty of the comic ritual. Joseph K. is expelled from the human order, first by being treated as an instrument, then by being killed like a dog; but the result of his expulsion is not, as it is in traditional comedy, the restoration of order—it is the realization of chaos. The comedy of these works turned against itself turns the joy of living into a fear of life.

Faulkner, creating Joe Christmas's stage as a chessboard to epitomize the fusion of the novel's dark determinism and absurd comedy, creates a world where his hero is drawn in and excluded from society, where he is forced to choose an identity but denied a choice, where every expression of life is a form of destruction, where heroic action is clownish. Like the first two stages, Faulkner's is governed by a wanton force, but his is both transcendent (in the form of the Chess Player) and immanent (in the form of Grimm and Hines, and in varying degrees most of the other characters). Faulkner too turns comedy against itself to evoke a fear of life, but in the end he realizes the redemptive possibilities of comedy and of foolishness.

In all the works of Flannery O'Connor terror is also achieved by comic devices that accentuate antipodal and irreconcilable realms. The principal device is to turn the world upside down. We end with a terrifying picture of reality, but the comic surprise and sustained use of the clown achieve a positive epiphany, a transvaluation of values, an affirmation of underlying order.

Burroughs and Nabokov turn the world upside down not to rediscover primal order but for Burroughs to disclose and for Nabokov to revel in chaos and destruction. Through his verbal and structural sabotage, the clownish narrator of *Lolita* causes us to see perversity as love, madness as sanity, obsession as freedom, destruction as creation; and, after the gratuitous manipulation of the *scène à faire*, he denies us the possibility of moral and epistemological judgment. With O'Connor we end with a fear of commonplace reality, mixed with a deep if transient joy not realized in the works discussed prior to hers. With Burroughs and Nabokov we also end with a feeling of joy; but this joy is a source of terror, for it comes from our collaboration with the satanic narrators.

In *Henderson the Rain King, Second Skin, Invisible Man, The Tin Drum,* and Beckett's trilogy terror is realized in varying degrees, and on various levels of social and psychological reality, by showing the world as a fun-house barrel of laughs, where every effort to retain or recapture a posture of human dignity adds to the capricious momentum and to the comic destruction. While Dostoyevsky ended his novel with the most sane human being a madman, Bellow, Hawkes, Ellison, Grass, and Beckett explore with more and more acumen a world that is totally mad.

All the writers I have discussed have achieved a terrifying picture of reality through means of low comedy and farce, different pictures through different means. The success of their comic devices is due to the inherent tendency of comedy to surprise, confuse, and mock. But there is more. Henri Bergson points out that an incident becomes comic when, despite the central moral concern, it calls attention to the body. Eric Bentley in his *Life of the Drama* emphasizes that the special humor in farce is due to "the abstractness of the violence," to the outrage without consequences. An important function of the comedy in the works I have discussed is to underscore the impotence of moral concern, and to heighten the sense of outrage not by denying the consequences but by connecting the outrage with consequences that are unexpected and irrelevant. They have also called attention to the material and animal dimensions of man and explored these dimensions with variety and profundity.

When comedy turns to terror the result is obscene. Shelley defined obscenity as the sin against the spiritual in nature, and John Addington Symonds, developing this point, concluded that obscenity is a "cynical or voluptuous isolation of what is animal in man, for special contemplation of the mind." Note this difference: in traditional comedy man is ridiculed by comparing him to the animal; in the obscene comedy of the Grotesque, where realms of nature are unnaturally crossed and fused, the animal in man is cynically or voluptuously isolated for the contemplation of the human mind, and, we should add, for the awful exercise of the human emotions. In his remarkable study of *Madness and Civilization* Michel Foucault focuses our attention on two important views of the animal in man. Discussing the change in the treatment of madmen that occurred in the eighteenth century, he observes that madmen had always been seen and treated as animals, but while in earlier times "animal metamorphosis" was the visible sign of divine or infernal powers—a sign of the Beyond—in the eighteenth century it "dispossesses man of what is specifically human . . . to establish him at the zero degree of his own nature." The two important points for our purposes are: 1) the change in attitude toward the animal in man, realized by a historical change in thought and behavior, and 2) the relation between the animal in man and madness, and, consequently, folly.

Myshkin having an epileptic fit at the Epanchin party, Gregor transformed into a huge insect, Pip seen as an element of the dark animalistic world of his novel, Joseph K. hungrily kissing Fräulein Bürstner and being killed like a dog, Hulga left in the loft without her artificial leg, Burroughs's homosexual sadist hanging a boy to excite his victim's last erection, Humbert Humbert foolishly making love to a dirty adolescent, Joe Christmas coming to Joanna Burden through the kitchen window, Henderson in his T-shirt and jockey shorts, Skipper being violated over a water keg by his first mate dressed in a grass skirt, Oskar and the nurse on the sharp fiber rug, ancient Macmann making love to the decrepit Moll, the Unnamable ducking his head into the jar to trick his proprietress—are different images of man at "the zero degree of his own nature." In each case man has been reduced to his zero degree by the forces of reality—hence the obscene comic terror.

Enid Welsford points out that the court jester came to an end in England with the death of Charles I and in France with the Revolution: "When the divinity that hedges a king was broken down the fool lost his freedom, his joke, and his reason for existence. . . . The King, the Priest, and the Fool all belong to the same régime, all belong essentially to a society shaped by belief in Divine order, human inadequacy, efficacious ritual; and there is no real place for any of them in a world increasingly dominated by the notions of the puritan, the scientist, and the captain of industry." Western man's attitude toward the animal, the fool, the madman changed with the secularization of his world; and it changed even more when he lost his faith in reason, when he saw his universe governed by capricious forces. The view of the animal, the fool, and the madman as representing some higher or lower Beyond was replaced by a view of these figures representing the zero degree of existence. While traditional comedy ridiculed this aberrant condition in the name of human possibility, the modern writer uses comedy to show the aberrant as the real; his comedy becomes a force of human reduction.

In his *Origins of Attic Comedy* Francis Cornford emphasizes that the primitive fertility ritual reenacted *both* the death of Winter and the resurrection of Spring, and that the primitive response must have included *simultaneously* the fear and sadness effected by the death and the joy inspired by the resurrection. E. K. Chambers reinforces Cornford's argument by pointing out that both the real or symbolic death of the hero and resurrection were elements of the medieval sword dance and mummers play, which preceded the second birth of Western drama. Related to this contradictory experience is an experience that is even more profoundly disturbing: it is based on the ultimate identity of the protagonist and antagonist. Cornford explains that while the nature of the form requires that the antagonist appear as "a purely evil power," whose function it is to "cause the passion and death of the good Spirit," the antagonist was in his former turn the good Spirit himself. In modern Thrace "the adversary is an exact double in name and dress of the hero."

The fertility ritual, which preceded the birth of drama in classical and medieval times, enabled primitive man to live with a view of the cosmos as terrifyingly irrational, and to discover its creative potential. The division of the ritual into tragedy and comedy worked to diminish the primal contradiction by separating it into rationally comprehensible and emotionally and ethically manageable categories, one based on the experience of death and evil, the other on resurrection and goodness. It is difficult for the modern mind, conditioned by the long tradition of this separation, to accept that the primitive ritual and response were enacted and felt as unities. Walter Kerr in *Tragedy and Comedy*, a book filled with provocatively intuitive insights, recognizes that the two forms treat essentially the same experience, but he is compelled to establish the chronological and emotional priority of tragedy—the pain gives birth to the laughter.

Conditioned also by a highly developed sense of irony, ambivalence, and relativity, the modern mind finds it difficult to comprehend the primitive unity. Not to feel the unity but to comprehend it. During a performance of Beckett we are conscious of the audience's spontaneous laughter, of its sympathy for Gogo and Didi and Hamm and Clov and Winnie and Krapp, of its positive joy in their tentative and irrelevant triumphs; but on leaving the theater one hears nothing but comments on the play's gloominess, coldness, and despair. In the theater the spectator responds immediately to almost every nuance of Beckett's expression; in the lobby he asks, "What was it supposed to mean?" We should exempt the New York theatergoer from these generalizations; he leaves the theater acclaiming Beckett's wit and ingenuity, he knows that the play does not mean but happens. Both of these responses are defenses against an unfathomable and almost unbearable revelation; they secure the spectator from ever feeling the play's full contradictory impact.

Like the primitive fertility ritual, the plays of Beckett are based on an experience of primal contradiction, which can only be comprehended by experiencing death and life, evil and goodness as a unity. Unlike the primitive ritual, Beckett's plays are calculated to reveal it as painful. This is the implicit basis for Robert Brustein's distinction between the traditional "theatre of communion" and the modern "theatre of revolt." And Wolfgang Kayser in his definitive and otherwise excellent study of *The Grotesque in Art and Literature* cannot bring himself to face it. After an extremely thorough investigation and a carefully substantiated argument, Kayser concludes: "In spite of all the helplessness and horror inspired by the dark forces which lurk in and behind our world and have power to estrange it, the truly artistic portrayal effects a secret liberation. The darkness has been sighted, the ominous powers discovered, the incomprehensible forces challenged. And thus we arrive at a final interpretation of the grotesque: AN ATTEMPT TO INVOKE AND SUBDUE THE DEMONIC ASPECTS OF THE WORLD." But while Kayser continually and convincingly shows us how the artists and writers of the Grotesque invoked the demons, he never demonstrates how they subdued them. This is because he cannot do so. The Grotesque differs from other forms of art in that it does not leave us with a sense of order or peace. And many modern writers, sensing or believing that this kind of peace is a lie, have revived the Grotesque as their mode of apprehending, representing, and exploring reality. Rather than dispel primal contradiction or make it bearable, they attempt to reveal it in its fullness. If there is a note of optimism, and I hope to show that there is, it is based on a profoundly humanistic faith in man's ability to achieve a kind of dignity and to discover the rich creative potentialities in a terrifyingly absurd world.

The term "absurd" is most often misused to designate a homogeneous experience, and it has been a major purpose of this study to emphasize that without order variety is infinite, that there are countless different experiences of absurdity. The full effect of external confusion and internal irrationality has been best achieved by the use of comic strategies detached from the comic world view: transformation, caricature, mistaken identity, collision, intrusion, turning the world upside down, patterning reality into irreconcilable realms of black and white, parodying the quest for meaning and unity, exploiting the madness of pure relativity. If primal contradiction is epitomized in the identity of good and evil, perhaps the most graphic device to evoke it is the double; hence we should recall the unsettling doubles in Myshkin and Rogozhin, Magwitch and Miss Havisham, Christmas and Brown, Hazel Motes and Enoch Emery, Humbert Humbert and Clare Quilty, Kafka's victim and assailant, and all the characters in Beckett's trilogy. And if to unsettle is the conscious or unconscious aim of the writers I have discussed, a powerful structural device is the schizophrenic or shifting point of view, employed in one manner or another in every work discussed. Another, and perhaps the most significant structural device, is the travesty of the marriage ritual.

Traditional comedy depends on the actual or symbolic marriage ritual to reconcile the opposite forces of the drama, just as it reconciles opposite elements of human nature, and, finally, as it brings into harmony the primal contradictions of existence. The comic device detached from the comic ritual as a whole is the joke that brings the fullest pain. Comedy turned against itself ends in a travesty of the marriage ritual. And this travesty is realized explicitly or symbolically in *The Idiot* when Myshkin and Rogozhin spend the night together alongside the dead Nastasya, in "The Metamorphosis" when the Samsa family is reunited after the death of their disgusting bug, in *Great Expectations* with the continual presence of Miss Havisham and in the initial ending which brings Pip and Estella together to realize the impossibility of their union, in *The Trial* when Joseph K. reaches his arms out to the first sign of human help and hope at the moment he is killed like a dog, in *Light in August* with the farcical union of Byron and Lena, in *Wise Blood* when the repentant landlady confesses her love to the dead blind man, in *Henderson the Rain King* with the comic giant carrying a Persian orphan and running, "leaping, pounding, and tingling" over the frozen ground of Newfoundland, in *Second Skin* with the birthday picnic in the graveyard.

The travesty of the marriage ritual, realized actually or symbolically or even implicitly in the acerbic use of the comic device, achieves its terror by evoking irrationality most fully, by dramatizing the impossibility of reconciliation or harmony. Baudelaire distinguishes between joy and laughter: "Joy is a unity whereas laughter is the revelation of a double, not to say a self-contradictory, sentiment." "Laughter is satanic, and, therefore, profoundly human . . . it is at once a sign of infinite grandeur and of infinite wretchedness: of infinite wretchedness by comparison with the Absolute Being who exists as an idea in Man's mind; of infinite grandeur by comparison with the animals. It is from the perpetual shock produced by these two infinities that laughter proceeds." We come back again to the fundamental human contradiction, expressed so powerfully and eloquently in *King Lear*, and, in varying ways, in each of the works I have discussed. I have been stressing the point that comedy has been used by the modern writer to reduce man to the zero degree of his nature, to make us feel the pain and terror of an irrational universe. But Baudelaire brings us back to the other dimension of laughter, to the point that the use of comedy, even when turned against itself, can not only reveal awful inevitability but infinite possibility. Cedric Whitman suggests that the Grotesque from the beginning has revealed such possibility. In his study of *Aristophanes and the Comic Hero*, he corrects Kayser's thesis by showing that in the literature from Homer to Virgil grotesque minglings of animal and human forms did not evoke a "vision of the alienated world, but of the world embraced in all its grandeur, the world of possibility, action, and transcendent power." He concludes that in early times the Grotesque could reveal both the "dangerous and incalculable forces" and "a human kinship with the burgeoning abundance of the demonic world; and the mummers dressed as goats or rams, known from the Athenian vases, which are an important source for the origin of comedy, were surely striving, in the full tide of their merriment, to embrace that abundance through the magic of animals."

At one extreme of the writers I have discussed is Franz Kafka, who does not sound a note of possibility; every one of Kafka's works shows that human striving leads to destruction, that the affirmation of life leads to devitalization and death. Dostoyevsky ameliorates the pessimism of *The Idiot* with his clear and deliberate overtones of Christ and Don Quixote, but these overtones derive more from an initial religious commitment than the discovery of possibility within the world of his novel. The intrinsic possibilities Dostoyevsky does reveal derive from the obstinate vitality of his clownish characters, and here is an important beginning. Underground Man consciously acclaims that capricious action is the final defense against being turned into a piano key or a puppet of deterministic forces. The spontaneous clownishness of almost every Dostoyevskian character, major and minor, is more convincingly affirmative than Dostoyevsky's religious motifs. Remember Lebyadkin's fable of the noble cockroach in *The Possessed*. He was dumped into a pig pail with a "stew" of flies and beetles, but would not complain: "Observe that," cried Lebyadkin triumphantly, "observe that he does not complain, and recognise his noble spirit!" Dostoyevsky and Dickens were masters at the kind of characterization that turns Bergson's formula for caricature on its head; in a world that is absurdly deterministic they bring to life the noble and vital human element within the mechanized puppet. Through their clowns they effect a laughter like that described by Baudelaire, inspired by the "shock" of the opposing infinities. And in varying ways each author I have discussed has evolved a similar characterization.

The value of clownishness is realized implicitly in such different writers as Flannery O'Connor, who, in the tradition of Plato's foolish Socrates and Erasmus's Christian Fool, affirms what conventional rationality denies; Nabokov, who, in the tradition of the *sottie* fool and the demons of the miracle plays, affirms life in an irrational but joyful destruction; Faulkner, who, in the tradition of the buffoon, affirms the resiliency of human nature in a deterministic and destructive world. With the hero's conscious acceptance of the role of clown and with his deliberate choice of this role in the tradition of Harlequin, the values of clownishness become explicit.

R. W. B. Lewis has defined this kind of character in the modern American novel as *pícaro* and pilgrim—an outlaw, literally and spiritually, who often reminds us of Charlie Chaplin, and who seems to be taking an "eccentric pilgrimage" through a mysterious and hostile world "toward some shrine of honor and value and belief." The shrine may remain out of sight, but it nevertheless gives a sense of purpose to his encounters and a kind of form to the novel he inhabits.

Lewis's description takes us back to the original *picaro* and pilgrim of American letters, Henry David Thoreau, and to a key idea in his essay "Walking" that may be developed into a surprisingly accurate definition of a literary hero who appeared in *Moby Dick* and *Huckleberry Finn*, and then skipped almost a century to capture the imaginations of the best writers of the mid-twentieth century. Thoreau began his essay by showing, in a traditionally romantic etymology, how the word "sauntering" derived from " 'idle people who roved about the country, in the Middle Ages, and asked charity, under pretense of going *à la Sainte Terre*,' to the Holy Land, till the children exclaimed, 'There goes a *Sainte-Terrer*,' a Saunterer, a Holy-Lander." What is distinctive about the "saunterer" is, first, that while he may appear to be a mere vagrant, this is only because he has no particular home but is equally at home anywhere ("sauntering" may also derive from *sans terre*); and, second, that he is indeed going on a pilgrimage, even a crusade, to his Holy Land, for this is the purpose of true sauntering. The saunterer, then, may be less vagrant than the man who sits at home all day, and "no more vagrant than the meandering river, which is all the while sedulously seeking the shortest course to the sea."

Saul Bellow's Augie March seems to saunter without direction all his life, now taking the path chosen for him by Grandma Lausch, now the one chosen by Einhorn, by Mrs. Renling, by Thea, by Stella, by Mintouchian. Even when he apparently chooses for himself, and joins the merchant marine, he is shipwrecked, lost at sea, and directed by the capricious winds and waves and the mad

Basteshaw who thinks he has the secret of life. Still, Augie manages to preserve his identity, as unformed as it may appear to us at any one time in the novel; and, as it turns out, the course he wanders is indeed his own. Einhorn tells him, "You've got *opposition* in you. You don't slide through everything. You just make it look so." What preserves Augie, what stimulates the opposition, is, as Augie finally tells us, "the *animal ridens* in me, the laughing creature, forever rising up." Augie's natural comic viewpoint enables him to accept life's hostility and absurdity and be at home wherever he is. When at last he calls himself "a sort of Columbus of those near-at-hand," he suggests that like the saunterer and like Columbus, he is on a voyage of discovery, that the particular goal is unknown, that the Holy Land or New World is himself.

And when Bellow's comic giant, Henderson, decides to leave his wife and children and pig farm and America for Africa, and, once there, to leave his friends and all the baggage of civilization, it is to *walk* into the interior caring nothing for a destination but only to go: far— "Oh, man! The farther the better." Once inside, he is jubilant, and tells us, "I had sensed from the first that I might find things here which were of old, which I saw when I was still innocent and have longed for ever since, for all my life—and without which *I could not make it.*" Henderson never really escapes society: memories of his wives, his children, his friends, his farm, the army are always with him; and an inherited sense of social responsibility involves him actively, if not always successfully, in the societies of the Arnewi and the Wariri. Nor does he ever escape himself. What Henderson finds in the depths of Africa is the image of his own irrational vitality. When he comes out of the jungle in his T-shirt and jockey shorts, carrying the lion cub that is supposed to contain the soul of the tribal chief he had become, it is not because he has decided on a particular destiny but for much the same reason that Thoreau came back from Walden Pond—he has several more lives to live. And it is also because he can ask: "What's the universe? Big. And what are we? Little. I therefore might as well be at home where my wife loves me. And even if she only seemed to love me, that too was better than nothing."

The hero of Ralph Ellison's *Invisible Man* spends the first part of his comic-nightmare life learning how to be at home in the world. He comes to realize that he is invisible, that no one, white or black, sees him as he really is, and that this is the condition of the Negro in America—indeed of man in the modern world. When he finally burns all the papers that have given him a factitious personality, from his high-school diploma to the note containing his new Brotherhood name, he renounces all visible signs of identity and accepts himself —as do Augie and Henderson—as a man who can saunter toward his Holy Land in a world that is both senseless and dangerous. While we never see him dramatically portrayed in his new posture, it is his new voice that gives the book its style, and that tells the hilarious and yet bitter tale.

Bellow's characters accept the role of clown. Ellison's hero chooses it and acts his role in the mental and verbal improvisation of his autobiography. Grass's Oskar carries the improvisation further, to the point that we cannot tell where the improvisation actually begins. Beckett's narrators carry the mental and verbal improvisation to the limits of the novelistic form.

Beckett also develops to its limits a mode of characterization that we observed in Dickens, Dostoyevsky, Faulkner, and O'Connor—pantomime. This mode of characterization is most evident in *Molloy*, where there is more emphasis on the physical world than in the other parts of the trilogy. "I took off my hat and looked at it. It is fastened, it has always been fastened, to my buttonhole, always the same buttonhole, at all seasons by a long lace. I am still alive then. That may come in useful. The hand that held the hat I thrust as far as possible from me and moved in an arc, to and fro. As I did so, I watched the lapel of my greatcoat and saw it open and close." Here we have the consummate image of man as a puppet, of man comically reduced to an object in a world of objects. Many readers stop here in their critical reaction to Beckett; but they miss the most important point. For Molloy is moving the hat himself. And he is watching his lapel open and close. Beckett has taken Dostoyevsky's figure of man as a piano key and has explored the imaginative possibilities of man, not escaping his situation by capricious action, but capriciously playing the key himself.

As the novel continues we watch Molloy communicating with his aged mother through a system of knocking on her head. We watch him on his bicycle: "I fastened my crutches to the cross-bar, one on either side, I propped the foot of my stiff leg (I forget which, now they're both stiff) on the projecting front axle, and I pedalled with the other . . . every hundred yards or so I stopped to rest my legs. . . . I didn't properly speaking get down off the machine, I remained astride it, my feet on the ground, my arms on the handle bars, my head on my arms, and I waited until I felt better." We see him "levering" himself forward on his crutches, "swinging slowly through the sullen air." We follow him as he observes his hands on the sheet: "they are a couple, they play with the sheet, love-play perhaps, trying to get up perhaps, one on top of the other. But it doesn't last, I bring them back, little by little, towards me, it's resting time." For several pages we witness his various attempts to distribute and circulate sixteen sucking stones throughout four pockets to achieve the maximum satisfaction from each stone. We follow him as one leg gets stiffer and the other shorter, as he pivots, props, and propels himself along. We see him stomp a charcoal burner: "I carefully chose the most favorable position, a few paces from the body, with my back of course turned to it. Then, nicely balanced on my crutches, I began to swing, backwards, forwards, feet pressed together, or rather legs pressed together, for how could I press my feet together, in the state they were? . . . I swung . . . in an ever widening arc, until I decided the moment had come and launched myself forward with all my strength and consequently, a moment later, backward, which gave the desired result." Even when he is finally forced to abandon "erect motion" we see him continue to improvise: "Flat on my belly, using my crutches like grapnels, I plunged them ahead of me into the undergrowth, and when I felt they had a hold, I pulled myself forward, with an effort of the wrists. . . . I even crawled on my back, plunging my crutches blindly behind me into the thickets. . . . I kept losing my hat, the lace had broken long ago, until in a fit of temper I banged it down on my skull with such violence that I couldn't get it off again. And if I had met any lady friends, if I had had any lady friends, I would have been powerless to salute them correctly."

Beckett has written two mimes for the stage, and has included pantomime direction that becomes more and more elaborate in his other plays; *Happy Days* requires that the actress memorize a detailed and intricate series of mime directions that is longer than the monologue itself. The singular effect of *Molloy* is in great part due to the many scenes that are written like pantomime scenarios. The effect of these scenarios, like the effect of a good stage mime, is carving into pure silence and pure space. Molloy tells us that "to restore silence is the role of objects." And to reduce the familiar world to silence and space is the first aim of Beckett's clowns. After this reduction, a new world is created that is at once familiar and strange.

On the ideal mime stage objects and people are created out of pure space; on a less ideal stage actual props are used, but, as Marcel Marceau once explained in a television interview, they are transformed into functional characters. The essence of an object, then, if it exists on the mime stage, is established in its reciprocal relationship to the mime. With nothing on the bare stage but a human body and perhaps a few props, the mime has the power to impart life and define existence.

The mime is a clown who achieves his unique success by turning his body into an instrument. During his long and arduous training the mime learns to analyze his body into all its component parts; then he learns to displace his center of balance from the inner ear, and finally to displace his center of orientation from the brain. The result is that each part of the body can receive a physical or emotional impact according to its own laws. And in the end the mime can fashion a totally new synthesis of parts and movements. When Marceau lifts a heavy dumbbell, he shows the separate effects of the strain on his head, neck, shoulders, arms, back, legs, and feet. The total effect is not that of a man realistically locked into the single effort of lifting a weight; we do not see a man confined by his burden and purpose. Rather we see the whole man affected physically and emotionally by the strain; we see a unique individual, composed of a great number of separate and even conflicting elements brought to life. And we are reminded of Pirandello's definition of the purpose of comic art: to reveal the conflicts and diversity in man.

Perhaps one reason that the clown has appealed to the Romantic imagination is that he demonstrates the ultimate Romantic affirmation. By deliberately turning himself into a puppet with innumerable conflicting parts, he frees himself to react most fully to his environment. By deliberately displacing his center of gravity and orientation from his head, he frees himself from the control of rational purpose, and he frees himself to create and define his environment. By turning himself into a machine, he achieves a final victory over the world of machines. This is what Molloy accomplishes when he moves his hat in an arc and watches his lapel follow and concludes that he is alive. And if we extend the principle of mime improvisation to the mental and emotional improvisation of Ellison's Invisible Man, Grass's Oskar, and Beckett's various narrators, we can explain how they achieve a sense of freedom and vitality even in the most extreme and desperate situations. For improvisation finally depends on the ability of the whole person to respond instantaneously and completely to a surprise cue. Man appears most alive when he is in a state of maximum alertness. He has the opportunity to be most alive and free when confronted with the maximum possibility of surprise. Baudelaire proclaims that "the Incarnate Word was never known to laugh. For Him who knows all things, whose powers are infinite, the comic does not exist." A comic view of the world, one which realizes and actuates all the surprises, is profoundly humanistic. Molloy, who is surprised at himself that he knows so well the story of his first love, dramatizes an important point. Improvisation is based on memory plus invention. Part of the surprise he evinces results from an awareness of a self that is different from the one he remembers. Improvisation is a joining of the old with the new. The surprise develops at the awesome juncture. In a world full of surprises, the world of the absurd, the clown—who reacts to a surprise instantaneously and completely, and who continually makes the juncture of the old with the new —is the hero.

The writers whom I have discussed have explored the

world of the clown by at least implicitly realizing that it is a stage in a many-ringed circus. Hence the importance of theatrical devices. The mechanical transformations of scene, the comic collisions, the implausible *scène à faire*, the uses of the caricature, the *alazon*, the *miles gloriosus*, the *eiron*, the balancing and doubling and endless multiplication, the travesty of the marriage ritual—are all appropriate to the stages of the clown.

The clown succeeds because of his moral and physical resiliency; he is diametrically opposed to Bergson's puppet. What gives the clown his resiliency, and hence his most human quality, is his genius for play. In a book called *Homo Ludens*, Johan Huizinga defines "play" as a completely voluntary and nonutilitarian activity, marked off from "ordinary life" by its own course, order, and meaning; and yet he shows it to be the basis of law, philosophy, art, myth, war, in short, of all the "great archetypal activities of human society." Most important, according to Huizinga, is that play becomes possible only "when an influx of *mind* breaks down the absolute determinism of the cosmos." It is important to emphasize that the influx of mind is not to the end of rational purpose or even of what is rationally conceived as man's best interest. The vitality of Socrates and Folly, of the medieval fools and demons, of Harlequin, of the clownish characters, and of the characters who choose the role of clown depends upon sheer playfulness. We are brought back to a strain of the humanistic tradition initiated by Archilochus, and to a heroic concept of man who can realize the full challenge of total freedom in "stringing together impossibilities."

Selected Bibliography

Appel, Alfred, Jr. "Lolita: The Springboard of Parody,"
    Wisconsin Studies in Contemporary Literature, VIII
    (Spring 1967), 204–41.
———. "Nabokov's Puppet Show," *The New Republic*,
    CLVI (January 14, 1967), 27–30, and (January 21, 1967),
    25–32.
Baudelaire, Charles. "The Essence of Laughter" in *The
    Essence of Laughter and Other Essays, Journals, and
    Letters*, ed. Peter Quennell, tr. Gerard Hopkins. New York,
    1956.
Beaumont, C. W. *The History of Harlequin*. London, 1926.
Beissner, Friedrich. *Der Erzähler Franz Kafka*. Stuttgart,
    1952.
Bentley, Eric. *The Life of the Drama*. New York, 1967.
Bergson, Henri. "Laughter" in *Comedy*. Garden City, N.Y.,
    1956.
Brustein, Robert. *The Theatre of Revolt: An Approach to
    the Modern Drama*. Boston and Toronto, 1964.
Burke, Kenneth. "The Grotesque" in *Attitudes Toward History*. New York, 1937.
Butler, Diana. "Lolita Lepidoptera," *New World Writing*,
    No. 16 (1960), pp. 58–84.
Chambers, E. K. *The Mediaeval Stage*. London, 1903.
Clark, James M. *The Dance of Death*. Glasgow, 1950.
Cohn, Dorrit. "Narrated Monologue: Definition of a Fictional Style," *Comparative Literature*, XVIII (Spring
    1966), 97–112.

158   STAGES OF THE CLOWN

Cohn, Ruby. *Samuel Beckett: The Comic Gamut.* New Brunswick, N.J., 1962.

——. "Terms of the Tragicomic Mixture," *Drama Survey,* V (Summer 1966), 186–91.

Cornford, Francis Macdonald. *The Origin of Attic Comedy.* London, 1914. (Republished in paperback by Doubleday-Anchor, 1961.)

Curtius, Ernst R. *European Literature and the Latin Middle Ages,* tr. Willard R. Trask. New York, 1953.

Disher, M. Willson. *Clowns and Pantomimes.* London, 1925.

Dostoyevsky, Fyodor. *The Notebooks for "The Idiot,"* ed. Edward Wasiolek, tr. Katharine Strelsky. Chicago and London, 1967.

Field, Andrew. *Nabokov: His Life in Art.* Boston and Toronto, 1967.

Foucault, Michel. *Madness and Civilization: A History of Insanity in the Age of Reason,* tr. Richard Howard. New York, 1965.

Friedman, Melvin, and Lewis A. Lawson, eds. *The Added Dimension: The Art and Mind of Flannery O'Connor.* New York, 1966.

Frye, Northrop. *Anatomy of Criticism.* Princeton, N.J., 1957.

Greenberg, Martin. "Kafka's 'Metamorphosis' and Modern Spirituality," *The Terror of Art: Kafka and Modern Literature.* New York, 1968, pp. 69–91. (First published in *Tri-Quarterly,* No. 6, pp. 5–20.)

Hassan, Ihab. "The Dismemberment of Orpheus," *American Scholar,* XXXII (Summer 1963), 463–84.

——. *The Literature of Silence: Henry Miller and Samuel Beckett.* New York, 1967.

——. *Radical Innocence: The Contemporary American Novel.* Princeton, N.J., 1961. (Republished in paperback by Harper and Row, 1966.)

Hawkes, John. "Notes on the Wild Goose Chase," *The Massachusetts Review,* III (Summer 1962), 784–88.

Heisenberg, Werner. *The Physicist's Conception of Nature,* tr. Arnold J. Pomerans. New York, 1958.

Hoffman, Frederick J. *The Mortal No: Death and the Modern Imagination*. Princeton, N.J., 1964.

Hollander, John. "The Perilous Magic of Nymphets" in *On Contemporary Literature*, ed. Richard Kostelanetz. New York, 1964.

Hughes, Robert. *Vladimir Nabokov*, a film made for National Educational Television, 1966.

Huizinga, Johan. *Homo Ludens: A Study of the Play-Element in Culture*. Boston, 1955.

Kaiser, Walter J. *Praisers of Folly: Erasmus, Rabelais, Shakespeare*. Cambridge, Mass., 1963.

Kayser, Wolfgang. *The Grotesque in Art and Literature*, tr. Ulrich Weisstein. Bloomington, Ind., 1963.

Kellett, E. E. "The Grotesque" in *Fashion in Literature: A Study of Changing Taste*. London, 1931.

Kerr, Walter. *Tragedy and Comedy*. New York, 1967.

Kott, Jan. *Shakespeare, Our Contemporary*, tr. Boleslaw Taborski. Garden City, N.Y., 1964.

Krieger, Murray. *The Tragic Vision: Variations on a Theme in Literary Interpretation*. New York, 1960.

Kurtz, Leonard P. *The Dance of Death and the Macabre Spirit in European Literature*. New York, 1934.

Lewis, R. W. B. *The Picaresque Saint: Representative Figures in Contemporary Fiction*. Philadelphia, 1959.

———. "Pícaro and Pilgrim" in *A Time of Harvest: American Literature, 1910–1960*, ed. Robert E. Spiller. New York, 1962.

———. *Trials of the Word*. New Haven and London, 1965.

McAlindon, T. "Comedy and Terror in Middle English Literature: The Diabolical Game," *The Modern Language Review*, LX (July 1965), 321–32.

McLuhan, Marshall. *Understanding Media: The Extensions of Man*. New York, 1964.

Nabokov, Vladimir. *Nikolai Gogol*. Norfolk, Conn., 1944.

Nicoll, Allardyce. *The World of Harlequin: A Critical Study of the Commedia dell-Arte*. Cambridge, Eng., 1963.

Niklaus, Thelma. *Harlequin; or, The Rise and Fall of a Bergamask Rogue*. New York, 1956.

O'Connor, Flannery. "A Collection of Statements," ed. Lewis A. Lawson in *The Added Dimension: The Art and Mind of Flannery O'Connor*, eds. Melvin J. Friedman and Lewis A. Lawson. New York, 1966.

——. "The Fiction Writer and His Country" in *The Living Novel*, ed. Granville Hicks. New York, 1962.

Parkes, Henry Bamford. "Metamorphosis of Leatherstocking" in *Literature in America*, ed. Philip Rahv. New York, 1957.

Pirandello, Luigi. "The Art of Humor," tr. John Patrick Pattinson, *The Massachusetts Review*, VI (Spring–Summer 1965), 515–20.

Robbe-Grillet, Alain. *Pour un nouveau roman*. Paris, 1963. (Republished as *For a New Novel: Essays on Fiction*, tr. Richard Howard. New York, 1966.)

Rovit, Earl H. "Ralph Ellison and the American Comic Tradition," *Wisconsin Studies in Contemporary Literature*, I (Fall 1960), 34–42.

Santayana, George. " 'The Comic Mask' and 'Carnival' " in *Soliloquies in England*. New York, 1922. (Reprinted in *Theories of Comedy*, ed. Paul Lauter. Garden City, N.Y., 1964.)

Sartre, Jean-Paul. "*Aminadab* or the Fantastic Considered as a Language" in *Literary and Philosophical Essays*, tr. Annette Michelson. New York, 1962.

Spilka, Mark. *Dickens and Kafka: A Mutual Interpretation*. Bloomington, Ind., 1963.

Swain, Barbara. *Fools and Folly During the Middle Ages and the Renaissance*. New York, 1932.

Symonds, John Addington. "Caricature, the Fantastic, the Grotesque" in *Essays, Speculative and Suggestive*. New York, 1894.

Sypher, Wylie. *Loss of the Self in Modern Literature and Art*. New York, 1962.

Tanner, Tony. "The New Demonology," *Partisan Review*, XXXIII (Fall 1966), 547–72.

Van Ghent, Dorothy. *The English Novel: Form and Function*. New York, 1953. (Republished in paperback by Harper and Row, 1961.)

Von Kleist, Heinrich. "Essay on the Puppet Theater," tr. Eugene Jolas, *Partisan Review*, XIV (January–February 1947), 67–72.

Walcutt, Charles C. *American Literary Naturalism: A Divided Stream*. Minneapolis, 1956.

Welsford, Enid. *The Fool: His Social and Literary History*. London, 1935. (Republished in paperback by Doubleday-Anchor, 1961.)

Whitman, Cedric H. *Aristophanes and the Comic Hero*. Cambridge, Mass., 1964.

Wilson, A. E. *Christmas Pantomime: The Story of an English Institution*. London, 1934.

———. *The Story of Pantomime*. London, 1949.

Wright, Thomas. *A History of Caricature and Grotesque in Literature and Art*. London, 1865.

Index